PRAYING GOD'S WILL

for My Son

LEE ROBERTS

OLIVER NELSON

THOMAS NELSON PUBLISHERS
Nashville

This book is dedicated to my son,
Lee Roberts, Jr.

Other books by Lee Roberts

Praying God's Will for My Daughter
Praying God's Will for My Husband
Praying God's Will for My Wife

Published in Nashville, Tennessee, by Oliver-Nelson Books, a division of Thomas Nelson, Inc.

The Bible version used in this publication is THE NEW KING JAMES VERSION. Copyright © 1979, 1980, 1982, Thomas Nelson, Inc., Publishers. Verses have been modified to fit the prayer format.

Printed in the United States of America.

Library of Congress Cataloging-in-Publication Data

Roberts, Lee, 1941–
    Praying God's will for my son / Lee Roberts.
        p.   cm.
    ISBN 0-8407-9175-5
    1. Parents—Prayer-books and devotions—English.   2. Boys—
Religious life.   3. Christian life—1960–   I. Title.
BV283.C5R64   1993
242′.845—dc20   93-9640
                                                                                        CIP

                    1 2 3 4 5 6 — 98 97 96 95 94 93

Contents

For Parents Only

As Christian parents, we have a solemn obligation to constantly, and on a day-by-day basis, lift up our son in prayer. We have a tremendous responsibility before God on his behalf. We are responsible before God for his spiritual, emotional, and physical well-being for as long as he is under our control. We are also responsible before God to give him our loving and prayerful support in order to nurture him on his journey to adulthood.

The question now becomes, "What do I pray?" As Christians, our role model for prayer must be Jesus. Jesus said, our son "shall not live by bread alone, but by every word that proceeds from the mouth of God" (Matthew 4:4). And the "sword of the Spirit . . . is the word of God" (Ephesians 6:17).

What should you pray for your son? Scripture is clear that you should pray God's word for him. At the same time, you must never forget that God is sovereign and that He is not obligated to a name-it-and-claim-it theology. God will always do what is best for your son. But at the same time you will do well to understand that when you pray God's word for your son, you are actually praying both the mind and the perfect will of God for him.

If you follow a systematic plan of praying God's will for your son, you will see dynamic growth take place in his life. He will become the son and the man God intended him to be.

1
ANGER

Heavenly Father, I thank You for all that You do for my son and me. During this time of being alone with You I ask You, in Jesus' name, to hear Your word as my prayers concerning any anger that may abide in my son. Your word is clear that anger does not produce the righteousness that You want in each of us. I petition You now, with Your very words, to remove any anger from my son that may be a stumbling block in his walk with You. Thank You, God, for answering this my prayer for my son. Amen.

**God, in accordance
with Your Word . . .**

I pray that my son will be swift to hear, slow
to speak, slow to wrath; for his wrath does
not produce the righteousness of God.

JAMES 1:19–20

I pray that the discretion of my son makes him slow to anger, and it is to his glory to overlook a transgression.

PROVERBS 19:11

———— ■ ————

I pray that my son will commit his way to You, LORD, and trust also in You, and You shall bring it to pass. You shall bring forth his righteousness as the light, and his justice as the noonday. I pray that he will rest in You, LORD, and wait patiently for You. I pray that he does not fret because of him who prospers in his way or because of the man who brings wicked schemes to pass. I pray that he will cease from anger, and forsake wrath; that he does not fret—it only causes harm.

PSALM 37:5–8

———— ■ ————

I pray that my son will not hasten in his spirit to be angry, for anger rests in the bosom of fools.

ECCLESIASTES 7:9

I pray that my son will let all bitterness, wrath, anger, clamor, and evil speaking be put away from him, with all malice. I pray also that he will be kind to others, tenderhearted, forgiving others, just as God in Christ also forgave him.

EPHESIANS 4:31–32

———— ■ ————

I pray that my son understands that a fool vents all his feelings, but a wise person holds his back.

PROVERBS 29:11

———— ■ ————

I pray that my son knows that being slow to anger is better than the mighty and ruling his spirit is better than taking a city.

PROVERBS 16:32

———— ■ ————

I pray that my son realizes that a person who is quick-tempered acts foolishly.

PROVERBS 14:17

I pray that if my son is angry, he will not sin. That he does not let the sun go down on his wrath.

EPHESIANS 4:26

———————— ■ ————————

I pray that my son will make no friendship with an angry person and with a furious person he does not go, lest he learn their ways and set a snare for his soul.

PROVERBS 22:24–25

———————— ■ ————————

I pray that my son always remembers that a soft answer turns away wrath, but a harsh word stirs up anger.

PROVERBS 15:1

ATTITUDE

Lord Jesus, I ask You now, using the very words that have been given to me in the Holy Scriptures, to make certain that my son always has an attitude of joy in You and an attitude and an expectancy that he can do all things through You who gives him Your strength to face the issues and problems of life. Thank You, Lord, for his happiness and his joy. In Your name I pray. Amen.

**God, in accordance
with Your Word . . .**

I pray that my son knows that he can do all things through Christ who strengthens him.

PHILIPPIANS 4:13

———— ■ ————

I pray that my son will not sorrow, for the joy of the LORD is his strength.

NEHEMIAH 8:10

I pray that my son understands what Jesus meant when He said, "My grace is sufficient for you, for My strength is made perfect in weakness."

2 CORINTHIANS 12:9

— ■ —

I pray that my son realizes that in all these things he is more than a conqueror through You who loved him.

ROMANS 8:37

— ■ —

I pray that my son will always love You, the Lord his God, with all his heart, with all his soul, with all his mind, and with all his strength and that he will love his neighbor as himself.

MARK 12:30–31

— ■ —

I pray that whatever my son does he does it heartily, as to You, Lord, and not to men.

COLOSSIANS 3:23

I pray that my son will remember whatever things are true, whatever things are noble, whatever things are just, whatever things are pure, whatever things are lovely, whatever things are of good report, if there is any virtue and if there is anything praiseworthy— that he will meditate on these things.

PHILIPPIANS 4:8

■

I pray that my son will remember that this is the day the LORD has made and that he will rejoice and be glad in it.

PSALM 118:24

3

CONDEMNED

Lord God, I come before You at this moment to ask You to keep in my son's mind at all times that there is no condemnation for those that are in Christ Jesus. Help him to know that if he trusts in Jesus he need not let Satan bring thoughts of doubt and condemnation to be in his mind. Thank You, Lord, for removing all such thoughts and feelings from my son. Thank You in Jesus' name. Amen.

God, in accordance
with Your Word . . .

I pray that there is therefore now no condemnation to my son who is in Christ Jesus, who does not walk according to the flesh, but according to the Spirit. For the law of the Spirit of life in Christ Jesus has made him free from the law of sin and death.

ROMANS 8:1–2

I pray that my son will draw near with a
true heart in full assurance of faith, having
his heart sprinkled from an evil conscience
and his body washed with pure water.

HEBREWS 10:22

———— ■ ————

I pray that my son always remembers that
You, the LORD his God, are gracious and
merciful, and will not turn Your face from
him if he returns to You.

2 CHRONICLES 30:9

———— ■ ————

I pray that my son knows that it was You,
God, who said that, "I, even I, am He who
blots out your transgressions for My own
sake."

ISAIAH 43:25

———— ■ ————

I pray that as far as the east is from the west,
so far have You removed my son's
transgressions from him.

PSALM 103:12

I pray that if my son is in You, Christ, he is a new creation; old things have passed away; behold, all things have become new.

2 CORINTHIANS 5:17

———— ■ ————

I pray that my son is blessed, whose transgression is forgiven, whose sin is covered.

PSALM 32:1

———— ■ ————

I pray, God, that You did not send Your Son into the world to condemn my son, but that my son through Him might be saved. He who believes in Him is not condemned.

JOHN 3:17–18

———— ■ ————

I pray that my son, who hears Your word, Jesus, and believes in Him who sent You has everlasting life, and shall not come into judgment, but has passed from death into life.

JOHN 5:24

I pray that You, God, will be merciful to my son's unrighteousness, and to his sins, and to his lawless deeds and that You remember them no more.

HEBREWS 8:12

■

I pray that my son will forsake any wicked ways and any unrighteous thoughts. Let him return to You, LORD, and You will have mercy on him and abundantly pardon him.

ISAIAH 55:7

■

I pray that my son has overcome Satan by the blood of the Lamb and by the word of his testimony.

REVELATION 12:11

■

I pray that my son remembers that Jesus Himself said, "Neither do I condemn you; go and sin no more."

JOHN 8:11

I pray that my son will acknowledge his sin to You, God, and his iniquity he has not hidden. I pray that he will confess his transgressions to You so You can forgive the iniquity of his sins.

PSALM 32:5

■

I pray that if my son will confess his sins, You, God, are faithful and just to forgive his sins and to cleanse him from all unrighteousness.

1 JOHN 1:9

■

I pray, God, that You will forgive my son's iniquity, and his sin You will remember no more.

JEREMIAH 31:34

4
CONFIDENCE

Lord Jesus, based upon God's word I call upon You to fill my son with confidence. Give him the spiritual confidence to know that whatever he asks in Your name he will receive. Fill him with the confidence that only You can give. Thank You for honoring Your word and my prayers. Amen.

**God, in accordance
with Your Word . . .**

I pray, God, that my son always remembers that it is You who justifies.

ROMANS 8:33

———— ■ ————

I pray that when my son passes through the waters, You will be with him; and through the rivers, they shall not overflow him. When he walks through the fire, he shall not be

burned, nor shall the flame scorch him. For
You are the LORD his God.

ISAIAH 43:2–3

———— ■ ————

I pray that this is the confidence that my
son has in You, Jesus, that if he asks anything
according to Your will, You hear him. And
if he knows that You hear him, whatever he
asks, he knows that he has the petitions that
he asked of You.

1 JOHN 5:14–15

———— ■ ————

I pray that when my son faces an obstacle
he always remembers that God has said that
it is "Not by might nor by power, but by My
Spirit."

ZECHARIAH 4:6

———— ■ ————

I pray that whatever my son asks in Jesus'
name, You will do it.

JOHN 14:14

I pray that You, the LORD God, are my son's strength.

HABAKKUK 3:19

———— ■ ————

I pray that my son will not cast away his confidence, which has great reward. For he has need of endurance, so that after he has done Your will, God, he may receive the promise.

HEBREWS 10:35–36

———— ■ ————

I pray that my son will be confident of this very thing, that You who have begun a good work in him will complete it until the day of Jesus Christ.

PHILIPPIANS 1:6

———— ■ ————

I pray that my son can do all things through Christ who strengthens him.

PHILIPPIANS 4:13

I pray that my son may boldly say: "The LORD is my helper; I will not fear. What can man do to me?"

HEBREWS 13:6

———— ■ ————

I pray that if my son's heart does not condemn him, he will have confidence toward You, God.

1 JOHN 3:21

———— ■ ————

I pray that if my son will wait on You, LORD, he shall renew his strength. He shall mount up with wings like eagles. He shall run and not be weary, he shall walk and not faint.

ISAIAH 40:31

5
CONFUSED

Heavenly Father, in the beautiful and precious name of Jesus, my Lord and my Savior, I ask You to remove all confusion from my son. Help him to know that Your word says You are the author of peace and not of confusion and that he is to lean on You and Your word and not his own understanding. Thank You, in Jesus' name, for honoring this my prayer for my wonderful and precious son. Amen.

God, in accordance
with Your Word . . .

I pray that my son will trust in You, LORD, with all his heart, and lean not on his own understanding. I pray that in all his ways he will acknowledge You, and You will direct his paths.

PROVERBS 3:5–6

I pray that You, God, will instruct my son
and teach him in the way he should go.

PSALM 32:8

———————— ■ ————————

I pray that my son has great peace because
he loves Your law, and nothing can cause
him to stumble.

PSALM 119:165

———————— ■ ————————

I pray that my son will always cast his
burdens on You, LORD, and You shall sustain
him.

PSALM 55:22

———————— ■ ————————

I pray that when my son passes through the
waters, You will be with him. And when he
passes through the rivers, they shall not
overflow him. When he walks through the
fire, he shall not be burned, nor shall the
flame scorch him. For You are the LORD his
God.

ISAIAH 43:2–3

I pray that my son will be anxious for nothing, but in everything by prayer and supplication, with thanksgiving, let his requests be made known to You, God, and the peace of God, which surpasses all understanding, will guard his heart and mind through Christ Jesus.

PHILIPPIANS 4:6–7

I pray that my son will always remember that God gives power to the weak, and to those who have no might He increases strength.

ISAIAH 40:29

I pray that my son knows that where envy and self-seeking exist, confusion and every evil thing will be there. But the wisdom that is from above is first pure, then peaceable, gentle, willing to yield, full of mercy and good fruits, without partiality and without hypocrisy.

JAMES 3:16–17

I pray that when my son feels confused he will remember and understand that You, God, are not the author of confusion but of peace.

1 CORINTHIANS 14:33

———— ■ ————

I pray, God, that You have not given my son a spirit of fear, but of power and of love and of a sound mind.

2 TIMOTHY 1:7

———— ■ ————

I pray that You, Lord God, will help my son; therefore he will not be disgraced.

ISAIAH 50:7

———— ■ ————

I pray that my son will not think it strange concerning the fiery trial which is to try him, as though some strange thing happened to him; but that he will rejoice to the extent

that he partakes of Christ's sufferings, that
when His glory is revealed, he may also be
glad with exceeding joy.

1 PETER 4:12–13

———— ■ ————

I pray that if my son lacks wisdom, let him
ask of You, God, who gives to all liberally
and without reproach, and it will be given
to him.

JAMES 1:5

6

COURAGE

Perfect God, grant my son the courage that only You can give. Help him to remember that You promised in Your word that he can do all things through Jesus and that he should never be afraid or discouraged or dismayed because You, his God, will be with him always. Thank You, God, in Jesus' name, for filling my son with courage. Amen.

God, in accordance
with Your Word . . .

I pray that my son will be persuaded that neither death nor life, nor angels nor principalities nor powers, nor things present nor things to come, nor height nor depth, nor any other created thing, shall be able to separate him from the love of God which is in Christ Jesus his Lord.

ROMANS 8:38–39

I pray that my son will always fear not, for You, God, are with him. I pray that he will not be dismayed, for You are his God. I pray that You will strengthen him and help him and that You will uphold him with Your righteous right hand.

ISAIAH 41:10

---■---

I pray that my son shall not die, but live, and declare the works of the LORD.

PSALM 118:17

---■---

I pray that You, the eternal God, are my son's refuge and that You will thrust out the enemy from before him.

DEUTERONOMY 33:27

---■---

I pray that my son can do all things through Christ who strengthens him.

PHILIPPIANS 4:13

I pray that my son will wait on You, LORD;
that he will be of good courage, and You
shall strengthen his heart.

PSALM 27:14

I pray that my son does not think it strange
concerning the fiery trial which is to try him,
as though some strange thing happened to
him; but that he will rejoice to the extent
that he partakes of Christ's sufferings, that
when His glory is revealed, he may also be
glad with exceeding joy.

1 PETER 4:12–13

I pray that when my son passes through the
waters, You will be with him; and through
the rivers, they shall not overflow him. When
he walks through the fire, he shall not be
burned, nor shall the flame scorch him. For
You are the LORD his God.

ISAIAH 43:2–3

I pray that while my son's weeping may endure for a night, joy comes to him in the morning.

PSALM 30:5

———— ■ ————

I pray that my son will be of good courage and that You shall strengthen his heart, for his hope is in You, LORD.

PSALM 31:24

———— ■ ————

I pray that my son will wait on You, LORD, and that he shall renew his strength. I pray that he shall mount up with wings like eagles; that he shall run and not be weary; that he shall walk and not faint.

ISAIAH 40:31

———— ■ ————

I pray that whatever things are true, whatever things are noble, whatever things are just, whatever things are pure, whatever things are lovely, whatever things are of good report, if there is any virtue and if there is anything praiseworthy—that my son will meditate on these things.

PHILIPPIANS 4:8

I pray that my son shall obtain joy and gladness and that sorrow and sighing shall flee away.

ISAIAH 51:11

I pray that my son will be anxious for nothing, but in everything by prayer and supplication, with thanksgiving, will let his requests be made known to You, God.

PHILIPPIANS 4:6

7

DELIVERANCE

Lord Jesus, today, at this very moment, I ask You to deliver my son from anything that is adversely afflicting him in any way. Help him to know the truth that comes only from You and Your word and to be set free from all that is upon him. Thank You, Jesus, for freeing my son and for filling him with joy and hope. Amen.

God, in accordance with Your Word . . .

I pray that my son shall know the truth, and the truth shall make him free.

JOHN 8:32

———— ■ ————

I pray that if You, Jesus, make my son free, he shall be free indeed.

JOHN 8:36

I pray that there is therefore now no condemnation to my son who is in Christ Jesus, who does not walk according to the flesh, but according to the Spirit. For the law of the Spirit of life in Christ Jesus has made him free from the law of sin and death.

ROMANS 8:1–2

■

I pray that my son does not believe every spirit, but that he tests the spirits, whether they are of You, God; because many false prophets have gone out into the world. I pray that by this he will know the Spirit of God: that every spirit that confesses that Jesus Christ has come in the flesh is of God.

1 JOHN 4:1–2

■

I pray that He who is in my son is greater than he who is in the world.

1 JOHN 4:4

I pray that my son has overcome Satan by the blood of the Lamb and by the word of his testimony.

REVELATION 12:11

8

DEPRESSED

Lord God, I pray to You now as always in Jesus' name. I ask You now in His name to remove any depression that may come upon my son at any time. Help him to know that if he will cry out to You that You will hear and deliver him. I ask You to honor Your word and deliver him from any depression that he may ever experience. In Jesus' name, Amen.

God, in accordance with Your Word . . .

I pray that my righteous son will cry out, and You will hear and deliver him out of all of his troubles.

PSALM 34:17

———— ■ ————

I pray, God, that You are the God of my son's strength.

PSALM 43:2

I pray that while my son's weeping may endure for a night, his joy comes in the morning.

PSALM 30:5

———— ■ ————

I pray that my son will wait on You, LORD. That he shall renew his strength. That he shall mount up with wings like eagles; that he shall run and not be weary and that he shall walk and not faint.

ISAIAH 40:31

———— ■ ————

I pray, God, that You will comfort my son in all his tribulation, that he may be able to comfort those who are in any trouble, with the comfort with which he himself is comforted by You.

2 CORINTHIANS 1:4

———— ■ ————

I pray that neither death nor life, nor angels nor principalities nor powers, nor things present nor things to come, nor height nor

depth, nor any other created thing, shall be
able to separate my son from Your love,
God, which is in Christ Jesus his Lord.

ROMANS 8:38–39

———— ■ ————

I pray that my son does not think it strange
concerning the fiery trial which is to try him,
as though some strange thing has happened
to him; but that he will rejoice to the extent
that he partakes of Christ's sufferings, so that
when His glory is revealed, he may also be
glad with exceeding joy.

1 PETER 4:12–13

———— ■ ————

I pray that whatever things are true,
whatever things are noble, whatever things
are just, whatever things are pure, whatever
things are lovely, whatever things are of good
report, if there is any virtue and if there is
anything praiseworthy—that my son will
meditate on these things.

PHILIPPIANS 4:8

I pray, God, that You will heal my son's broken heart and bind up his wounds.

PSALM 147:3

■

I pray that my son will fear not, for You are with him. That he will not be dismayed, for You are his God. I pray that You will strengthen him; that You will help him and that You will uphold him with Your righteous right hand.

ISAIAH 41:10

■

I pray that my son will always pray and not lose heart.

LUKE 18:1

■

I pray that my son will not sorrow, for the joy of the LORD is his strength.

NEHEMIAH 8:10

I pray that my son will humble himself under the mighty hand of God, that You may exalt him in due time. I pray that he will cast all his cares upon You, for You care for him.

1 PETER 5:6–7

9

DESERTED BY LOVED ONES

Heavenly Father, I plead with You at this moment to honor Your word and set my son on high. Your word has promised that You will never leave him nor forsake him, no matter what his loved ones might do. He needs You now. Draw him close to You and carry his burdens for him. In Jesus' name I pray. Amen.

God, in accordance with Your Word . . .

I pray that because You have set Your love upon my son, therefore You will deliver him; You will set him on high, because he has known Your name. I pray that he shall call upon You, and You will answer him; You will be with him in trouble; You will deliver him and honor him. That with long life You will satisfy him, and show him Your salvation.

PSALM 91:14–16

I pray, God, that You will not forsake my
son nor destroy him.

DEUTERONOMY 4:31

———— ■ ————

I pray that You, God, will hear my son and
that You will not forsake him.

ISAIAH 41:17

———— ■ ————

I pray that my son will cast all his cares upon
You, God, for You care for him.

1 PETER 5:7

———— ■ ————

I pray that while my son is hard pressed on
every side, yet he is not crushed; he is
perplexed, but not in despair; persecuted,
but not forsaken; struck down, but not
destroyed—always carrying about in his
body the dying of the Lord Jesus, that the
life of Jesus also may be manifested in his
body.

2 CORINTHIANS 4:8–10

I pray that my son will no longer be termed Forsaken and You will delight in him.

ISAIAH 62:4

———— ■ ————

I pray that because my son knows Your name, God, he will put his trust in You; for You, LORD, have not forsaken those who seek You.

PSALM 9:10

———— ■ ————

I pray that if even I forsake my son that You will take care of him.

PSALM 27:10

———— ■ ————

I pray that my son will be taught to observe all things that Jesus has commanded and that he knows that You are with him always, even to the end of the age.

MATTHEW 28:20

I pray that my son always remembers that
You will not forget him.

ISAIAH 49:15

■

I pray that my son's hope is in You, God,
and that he shall yet praise You, the help
of his countenance and his God.

PSALM 43:5

■

I pray that my son will be strong and of good
courage. That he will not fear nor be afraid;
for You, the LORD his God, are the One who
goes with him. I know that You will not leave
him nor forsake him.

DEUTERONOMY 31:6

■

I pray that You will not forsake my son, for
Your great name's sake, because it has
pleased You to make him one of Your
people.

1 SAMUEL 12:22

10

DISCOURAGED

Perfect God, in Jesus' name I ask You to remove from my son any discouragement that he may be feeling at this time in his life. Teach him what Your word means when it says to wait on You, and to be of good courage and that You, God, will strengthen him. Thank You for hearing and honoring Your words. Amen.

**God, in accordance
with Your Word . . .**

I pray that my son will wait on You, LORD;
that he will be of good courage, and that
You will strengthen his heart.

PSALM 27:14

---■---

I pray that my son will be of good courage
and that You, God, shall strengthen his heart.

PSALM 31:24

I pray that my son shall obtain joy and
gladness and that sorrow and sighing shall
flee away.

ISAIAH 51:11

———— ■ ————

I pray that my son will not cast away his
confidence, which has great reward. For he
has need of endurance, so that after he has
done Your will, God, he may receive his
promise.

HEBREWS 10:35–36

———— ■ ————

I pray that my son is confident of this very
thing, that You, God, who has begun a good
work in him will complete it until the day
of Jesus Christ.

PHILIPPIANS 1:6

———— ■ ————

I pray that my son does not grow weary
while doing good, for in due season he shall
reap if he does not lose heart.

GALATIANS 6:9

I pray that in everything my son will be anxious for nothing, but in everything by prayer and supplication, with thanksgiving, lets his request be made known to You, God; and Your peace, which surpasses all understanding, will guard his heart and mind through Christ Jesus.

PHILIPPIANS 4:6–7

I pray, God, that though my son walks in the midst of trouble, You will revive him. You will stretch out Your hand against the wrath of his enemies. I pray that with Your right hand You will save him.

PSALM 138:7

I pray that my son will greatly rejoice, though now for a little while, if need be, he may be grieved by various trials. I pray that the genuineness of his faith, being much more precious than gold that perishes, though it is tested by fire, may be found to praise, honor, and glory at the revelation of Jesus Christ, whom having not seen, he loves. Though now he does not see Him, yet believing, he rejoices with joy inexpressible and full of glory, receiving the end of his faith—the salvation of his soul.

1 PETER 1:6–9

———— ■ ————

I pray that my son will not let his heart be troubled. That he will believe in You, God, and also in Jesus.

JOHN 14:1

———— ■ ————

I pray that while my son is hard pressed on every side, he is not crushed; he is perplexed, but not in despair; persecuted, but not forsaken; struck down, but not destroyed—always carrying about in his body the dying of the Lord Jesus, that the life of Jesus also may be manifested in his body.

2 CORINTHIANS 4:8–10

11
DISSATISFIED

Lord Jesus, through the power of Your perfect and error-free word I call upon You to replace any dissatisfaction in my son's life with joy, hope, and happiness. Your word says his soul will be satisfied and he shall have every good thing. Through my faith and the authority of Your word I now pray Your word for my son and ask that You hear and honor these words from Your word in the Bible. Thank You for hearing my prayers. Amen.

God, in accordance
with Your Word . . .

I pray that my son will be satisfied with good by the fruit of his mouth.

PROVERBS 12:14

■

I pray that because my son seeks You, LORD, he shall not lack any good thing.

PSALM 34:10

I pray that my son will bless You, LORD, with all that is within him and that he will forget not all Your benefits. I pray that he will not forget who forgives all his iniquities and who heals all his diseases. I pray that he will not forget who redeems his life from destruction and who crowns him with lovingkindness and tender mercies and who satisfies his mouth with good things, so that his youth is renewed like the eagle's.

PSALM 103:1–5

———————— ■ ————————

I pray, God, that You will satisfy my son's longing soul, and fill his hungry soul with goodness.

PSALM 107:9

———————— ■ ————————

I pray that my son will trust and not be afraid; for You, God, are his strength and his song. You have become his salvation.

ISAIAH 12:2

I pray that my son can do all things through Christ who strengthens him.

PHILIPPIANS 4:13

---■---

I pray that my son's soul shall be satisfied as with marrow and fatness, and his mouth shall praise You with joyful lips.

PSALM 63:5

---■---

I pray that my son will delight himself in You, LORD, and You shall give him the desires of his heart.

PSALM 37:4

---■---

I pray that You, God, who supplies seed to the sower and bread for food, will supply and multiply the seed my son has sown and increase the fruits of his righteousness.

2 CORINTHIANS 9:10

12

DISTRESS / SADNESS

God in heaven, You have promised the comfort of the Holy Spirit to us in times such as this. I ask You for a special comforting for my son. Your word says that while sadness may come upon him that his joy will return in the morning. I pray this, Your word, for my son. Remove his distress. Take his sadness. And honor these Your words that I am about to pray. Thank You in Jesus' name. Amen.

God, in accordance
with Your Word . . .

I pray that my son has done justice and righteousness and that You will not leave him to his oppressors.

PSALM 119:121

———— ■ ————

I pray that while my son may be despised, he does not forget Your precepts.

PSALM 119:141

I pray that while trouble and anguish have overtaken my son, Your commandments are his delights. The righteousness of Your testimonies is everlasting. I pray that You will give him understanding, and he shall live.

PSALM 119:143–144

I pray that in righteousness my son shall be established. That he shall be far from oppression, for he shall not fear; and from terror, for it shall not come near him.

ISAIAH 54:14

I pray that You, God, will strengthen my son according to Your word.

PSALM 119:28

It is good for my son that he has been afflicted so that he may learn from Your statutes.

PSALM 119:71

I pray that You, God, will consider my son's affliction and deliver him, for he does not forget Your law. I pray that You will plead his cause and redeem him. Revive him according to Your word.

PSALM 119:153–154

I pray that my son has great peace because he loves Your law, God, and nothing causes him to stumble.

PSALM 119:165

I pray that if my son has gone astray like a lost sheep, that You, God, will seek him, Your servant, and not let him forget Your commandments.

PSALM 119:176

I pray that my son will always pray, "Blessed be the Lord," who daily loads him with benefits.

PSALM 68:19

I pray, God, that You will bring my son up out of a horrible pit and out of the miry clay. Set his feet upon a rock and establish his steps.

PSALM 40:2

I pray that You, God, are my son's refuge and strength, a very present help in trouble and that he will not fear.

PSALM 46:1–2

I pray that since Your name, LORD, is a strong tower, that my righteous son runs to it and is safe.

PROVERBS 18:10

I pray that my son will let not his heart be troubled and that he will always believe in God and in Jesus.

JOHN 14:1

I pray that my son will not sorrow, for the joy of the LORD is his strength.

NEHEMIAH 8:10

———— ■ ————

I pray that my son will always live with the realization that his Lord is faithful and will establish him and guard him from the evil one.

2 THESSALONIANS 3:3

13
DON'T UNDERSTAND GOD

Lord God, the words that I am about to pray are Your words. Hear them please and honor them. Help my son to understand that because Your thoughts are often higher than his thoughts that he may not always understand Your thoughts and Your way. Remind him of Your promise that if he will call upon You, You will tell him great and unsearchable things that he does not know. I now pray Your word to You in Jesus' name. Amen.

God, in accordance
with Your Word . . .

I pray that You, God, will help my son to understand that Your thoughts are not his thoughts, nor are his ways Your ways. That he will understand that as the heavens are higher than the earth, so are Your ways higher than his ways, and Your thoughts higher than his thoughts.

ISAIAH 55:8–9

I pray that my son will call to You, God, and
that You will answer him and show him great
and mighty things, which he does not know.

JEREMIAH 33:3

———— ■ ————

I pray that as for You, God, Your way is
perfect. The word of the Lord is proven; You
are a shield to my son who trusts in You.

PSALM 18:30

———— ■ ————

I pray, God, that You will perfect that which
concerns my son and that Your mercy, O
Lord, endures forever.

PSALM 138:8

———— ■ ————

I pray that You, God, will make an
everlasting covenant with my son, that You
will not turn away from doing him good;
but that You will put Your fear in his heart
so that he will not depart from You.

JEREMIAH 32:40

I pray that if You, God, are for my son, who can be against him?

ROMANS 8:31

———— ■ ————

I pray that in all things my son is more than a conqueror through You who loved him.

ROMANS 8:37

———— ■ ————

I pray that my son will pursue the knowledge of the LORD.

HOSEA 6:3

———— ■ ————

I pray that no temptation has overtaken my son except such as is common to man; but You, God, are faithful, who will not allow him to be tempted beyond what he is able, but with the temptation You will also make the way of escape, that he may be able to bear it.

1 CORINTHIANS 10:13

I pray that my son will hold fast the confession of his hope without wavering, for You, God, who promised are faithful.

HEBREWS 10:23

———— ■ ————

I pray that all things work together for good to my son who loves You, God, to him who was called according to Your purpose.

ROMANS 8:28

———— ■ ————

I pray that my son will cast his burden on You, LORD, and You shall sustain him.

PSALM 55:22

———— ■ ————

I pray that my son will fear not, for You, God, are with him. That he will be not dismayed, for You are his God. That You will strengthen him and help him. That You will uphold him with Your righteous right hand.

ISAIAH 41:10

I pray that while many are the afflictions of my righteous son, You, LORD, deliver him out of them all.

PSALM 34:19

———— ■ ————

I pray that my son does not think it strange concerning the fiery trial which is to try him, as though some strange thing happened to him; but that he will rejoice to the extent that he partakes of Christ's sufferings, that when His glory is revealed, he may also be glad with exceeding joy.

1 PETER 4:12–13

14

DOUBTING GOD

Heavenly Father, today I pray the power of Your perfect word to remove any doubts about You that my son might have. Your word says that Your way is perfect and Your word is proven. Use Your Holy Spirit to impart Your perfection to my son and to remove any doubts that he may have now or at any time in his life. Help him to believe and not doubt. In Jesus' name I pray. Amen.

God, in accordance with Your Word . . .

I pray that because Your way is perfect and Your word is proven, that You, God, are a shield to all who trust in You.

PSALM 18:30

I pray, God, that my son will always remember that Your hand is not shortened

so that it cannot save; nor Your ear heavy,
that it cannot hear.

ISAIAH 59:1

■

I pray that You, Lord, are not slack
concerning Your promise, as some count
slackness, but are longsuffering toward my
son, not willing that he should perish but
that he should come to repentance.

2 PETER 3:9

■

I pray, God, that my son is aware that You
have said Your counsel shall stand, and You
will do all Your pleasure. Indeed, You have
spoken it and You will also bring it to pass.
You have purposed it and You will also do
it.

ISAIAH 46:10–11

■

I pray that my son knows that He who calls
him is faithful, who also will do it.

1 THESSALONIANS 5:24

I pray that my son does not seek what he should eat or what he should drink, nor have an anxious mind. For all these things the nations of the world seek after, and You, his Father, know that he needs these things. I pray that he will seek the kingdom of God, and all these things shall be added to him.

LUKE 12:29–31

———— ■ ————

I pray that whatever things my son asks when he prays, that he will believe that he will receive them, and he will have them.

MARK 11:24

———— ■ ————

I pray that my son will always remember that You, God, have declared that, "So shall My word be that goes forth from My mouth; it shall not return to Me void, but it shall accomplish what I please, and it shall prosper in the thing for which I sent it."

ISAIAH 55:11

I pray that my son knows that faith comes
by hearing, and hearing by the word of God.

ROMANS 10:17

---■---

I pray that my son does not think it strange
concerning the fiery trial which is to try him,
as though some strange thing happened to
him. But that he rejoices to the extent that
he partakes of Christ's sufferings, that when
His glory is revealed, he may also be glad
with exceeding joy.

1 PETER 4:12–13

15

EMOTIONALLY UPSET

Jesus, I am here to ask You to give great peace to my son because he loves You so much. As Your word says, give him a sound mind and a peace that passes all understanding. Let him be anxious for nothing. Thank You, Jesus, for honoring Your word in this important time in my son's life. Amen.

God, in accordance with Your Word . . .

I pray that my son will have great peace because he loves Your law, and nothing causes him to stumble.

PSALM 119:165

———— ■ ————

I pray that because my son believes in You, God, he will by no means be put to shame.

1 PETER 2:6

I pray that You, God, will help my son;
therefore he will not be disgraced. He can
set his face like a flint and know that he will
not be ashamed.

ISAIAH 50:7

———— ■ ————

I pray that my son will be anxious for
nothing, but in everything by prayer and
supplication, with thanksgiving, will let his
requests be made known to You, God; and
Your peace, God, which surpasses all
understanding, will guard his heart and mind
through Christ Jesus.

PHILIPPIANS 4:6–7

———— ■ ————

I pray that my son will cast his burden on
You, LORD, and that You shall sustain him.

PSALM 55:22

———— ■ ————

I pray that my son will fear not, for You,
God, are with him. That he be not dismayed,

for You are his God. I pray that You will strengthen him and help him and that You will uphold him with Your righteous right hand.

ISAIAH 41:10

■

I pray that my son will realize that You, God, are not the author of confusion but of peace.

1 CORINTHIANS 14:33

■

I pray that my son knows that where envy and self-seeking exist, confusion and every evil thing will be there. I pray that he will also know that the wisdom that is from above is first pure, then peaceable, gentle, willing to yield, full of mercy and good fruits, without partiality and without hypocrisy and that the fruit of righteousness is sown in peace by those who make peace.

JAMES 3:16–18

I pray that You, God, have not given my son
a spirit of fear, but of power and of love and
of a sound mind.

2 TIMOTHY 1:7

———— ■ ————

I pray that while my son's weeping may
endure for a night, his joy comes in the
morning.

PSALM 30:5

———— ■ ————

I pray that when my son passes through the
waters, You, God, will be with him. And
when he passes through the rivers, they
shall not overflow him. I pray that when he
walks through the fire, he shall not be
burned, nor shall the flame scorch him.
You are the LORD his God.

ISAIAH 43:2–3

———— ■ ————

I pray that You, God, will heal my son's
broken heart and bind up his wounds.

PSALM 147:3

I pray that You, God, will comfort my son
in all his tribulation, that he may be able
to comfort those who are in any trouble,
with the comfort with which he himself is
comforted by You.

2 CORINTHIANS 1:4

———— ■ ————

I pray that whatever things are true,
whatever things are noble, whatever things
are just, whatever things are pure, whatever
things are lovely, whatever things are of good
report, if there is any virtue and if there is
anything praiseworthy—that my son will
meditate on these things.

PHILIPPIANS 4:8

———— ■ ————

I pray that neither death nor life, nor angels
nor principalities nor powers, nor things
present nor things to come, nor height nor
depth, nor any other created thing, shall be
able to separate my son from the love of
God which is in Christ Jesus his Lord.

ROMANS 8:38–39

16

FAITH

Father God, in the name of Your Son, Jesus, I pray to You for my son. Increase his faith. Help him to remember that You said he is to walk by faith and not by sight. Hear and answer Your word now concerning my son's faith. Thank You in Jesus' name. Amen.

**God, in accordance
with Your Word . . .**

I pray that You, Lord, will increase my son's faith.

LUKE 17:5

———— ■ ————

I pray that my son's faith comes by hearing, and hearing by the word of God.

ROMANS 10:17

I pray that my son will walk by faith and
not by sight.

2 CORINTHIANS 5:7

———— ■ ————

I pray that my son will have a pure heart, a
good conscience, and sincere faith.

1 TIMOTHY 1:5

———— ■ ————

I pray that my son will always remember
that faith is the substance of things hoped
for and the evidence of things not seen.

HEBREWS 11:1

———— ■ ————

I pray that my son remembers that faith by
itself, if it does not have works, is dead.

JAMES 2:17

———— ■ ————

I pray that my son will always have faith
and a good conscience.

1 TIMOTHY 1:19

I pray that my son will constantly take the shield of faith with which he will be able to quench all the fiery darts of the wicked one.

EPHESIANS 6:16

———— ■ ————

I pray that my son will put on the breastplate of faith and love, and as his helmet the hope of salvation.

1 THESSALONIANS 5:8

———— ■ ————

I pray that my son will fight the good fight of faith, that he will lay hold on eternal life, to which he was also called.

1 TIMOTHY 6:12

———— ■ ————

I pray that my son will draw near with a true heart in full assurance of faith and that he will have his heart sprinkled from an evil conscience and his body washed with pure water.

HEBREWS 10:22

I pray that my son understands that without
faith it is impossible to please You, God, and
that for him to come to You he must believe
that You are and that You are a rewarder
of those who diligently seek You.

HEBREWS 11:6

———— ■ ————

I pray that my son will be just and will live
by faith.

HABAKKUK 2:4

———— ■ ————

I pray that my son will remember that
Abraham believed God, and it was
accounted to him for righteousness.

ROMANS 4:3

———— ■ ————

I pray that my son, having been justified by
faith, will have peace with You, God, through
his Lord Jesus Christ.

ROMANS 5:1

I pray that my son will count all things as a loss for the excellence of the knowledge of Christ Jesus his Lord, for whom he has suffered the loss of all things, and count them as rubbish, that he may gain Christ and be found in Him, not having his own righteousness, which is from the law, but that which is through faith in Christ, the righteousness which is from God by faith; that he may know Him and the power of His resurrection, and the fellowship of His sufferings, being conformed to His death.

PHILIPPIANS 3:8–10

■

I pray that my son will be just and will live by faith.

HEBREWS 10:38

■

I pray that my son shall believe in You, the LORD his God, and that he shall be established. I pray also that he will believe Your prophets and he shall prosper.

2 CHRONICLES 20:20

I pray that according to my son's faith, it
will be to him.

MATTHEW 9:29

———— ■ ————

I pray that my son will have faith as a
mustard seed and he will say to his
mountain, "Move from here to there," and
it will move; and nothing will be impossible
for him.

MATTHEW 17:20

———— ■ ————

I pray that my son will have faith in You,
God.

MARK 11:22

———— ■ ————

I pray for my son the righteousness of You,
God, which is through faith in Jesus Christ
on him who believes.

ROMANS 3:22

I pray, God, that in Your forbearance You have passed over my son's sins that were previously committed.

ROMANS 3:25

I pray that my son will remember that if he has the gift of prophecy, and understands all mysteries and all knowledge, and though he has all faith, so that he can remove mountains, but has not love, he is nothing.

1 CORINTHIANS 13:2

I pray that my son will watch and that he will stand fast in the faith and that he will be brave and strong.

1 CORINTHIANS 16:13

I pray that my son will examine himself as to whether he is in the faith and that he will test himself.

2 CORINTHIANS 13:5

I pray that my son knows that he is not justified by the works of the law but by faith in Jesus Christ.

GALATIANS 2:16

I pray that my son has been crucified with Christ. That it is no longer he who lives, but Christ who lives in him. And that the life which he now lives in the flesh he lives by faith in the Son of God, who loves him and gave Himself for him.

GALATIANS 2:20

I pray that the sharing of my son's faith may become effective by the acknowledgment of every good thing which is in him in Christ Jesus.

PHILEMON 1:6

I pray that it is by faith that my son understands that the worlds were framed by the word of God, so that the things which are seen were not made of things which are visible.

HEBREWS 11:3

———— ■ ————

I pray that my son will always look unto Jesus, the author and finisher of his faith, who for the joy that was set before Him endured the cross, despising the shame, and has sat down at the right hand of the throne of God.

HEBREWS 12:2

———— ■ ————

I pray that my son understands that as the body without the spirit is dead, so faith without works is dead also.

JAMES 2:26

———— ■ ————

I pray that my son will realize that if he does not believe he shall not be established.

ISAIAH 7:9

I pray that my son knows the Holy Scriptures, which are able to make him wise for salvation through his faith which is in Christ Jesus.

2 TIMOTHY 3:15

I pray that my son will fight the good fight; that he will finish the race; and that he will keep the faith.

2 TIMOTHY 4:7

17

FEAR

God, I pray that You remove any and all fears my son may be harboring either now or in the future. I ask You to remember that my prayers are actually Your words on the subject of fear. Please honor Your perfect and error-free word and remove any and all fears now and forever in my son. Thank You, God, for hearing my prayers in Jesus' name. Amen.

God, in accordance with Your Word . . .

I pray that Your truth, God, shall be my son's shield and buckler and that he shall not be afraid.

PSALM 91:4–5

———— ■ ————

I pray that no evil shall befall my son.

PSALM 91:10

I pray that my son will not be afraid of sudden terror, nor of trouble from the wicked when it comes. I pray that You, LORD, will be his confidence and will keep his foot from being caught.

PROVERBS 3:25–26

———— ■ ————

I pray that in righteousness my son shall be established. He shall be far from oppression, for he shall not fear. And from terror, for it shall not come near him.

ISAIAH 54:14

———— ■ ————

I pray that in You, God, my son will put his trust and that he will not be afraid.

PSALM 56:11

———— ■ ————

I pray that my son knows that You, God, have not given him a spirit of fear, but of power and of love and of a sound mind.

2 TIMOTHY 1:7

I pray that my son did not receive the spirit
of bondage again to fear, but that he
received the Spirit of adoption by whom
he cries out, "Abba, Father."

ROMANS 8:15

■

I pray that in my son there is no fear in love;
because perfect love casts out fear.

1 JOHN 4:18

■

I pray that You, God, will give Your angels
charge over my son, to keep him in all his
ways.

PSALM 91:11

■

I pray that though my son walks through
the valley of the shadow of death, he will
fear no evil; for You, God, are with him. Your
rod and Your staff, they comfort him.

PSALM 23:4

I pray that my son will be of good courage
and that You, God, shall strengthen his heart,
for his hope is in the LORD.

PSALM 31:24

———— ■ ————

I pray that my son receives the peace that
You, Jesus, have left with him, the peace You
gave to him. Let not his heart be troubled,
neither let it be afraid.

JOHN 14:27

———— ■ ————

I pray that You, LORD, are my son's light and
his salvation. Whom shall he fear? Though
an army may encamp against him, his heart
shall not fear. In this he will be confident.

PSALM 27:1, 3

———— ■ ————

I pray that You, Lord, are my son's helper
and that he will not fear.

HEBREWS 13:6

I pray that if You, God, are for my son, who can be against him? Who shall separate him from the love of Christ? Shall tribulation, or distress, or persecution, or famine, or nakedness, or peril, or sword? I pray that in all these things he is more than a conqueror through Him who loved him. For I am persuaded that neither death nor life, nor angels nor principalities nor powers, nor things present nor things to come, nor height nor depth, nor any other created thing, shall be able to separate my son from Your love, God, which is in Christ Jesus his Lord.

ROMANS 8:31, 35, 37–39

18
FINANCIAL PROBLEMS

Heavenly Father, it is not Your will that my son should have to contend unnecessarily with financial problems. Because I believe strongly in Your word, I present to You as my prayers for my son Your very words on this subject. Please honor Your word and release him from any and all financial problems in his life. I pray Your words in Jesus' name. Amen.

God, in accordance with Your Word . . .

I pray that my son may prosper in all things and be in health, just as his soul prospers.

3 JOHN 1:2

———■———

I pray that You, LORD, are my son's shepherd and that he shall not want.

PSALM 23:1

I pray that my son will seek You, LORD, and not lack any good thing.

PSALM 34:10

———— ■ ————

I pray that all these blessings shall come upon my son and overtake him, because he obeys the voice of the LORD his God. He shall be blessed in the city, and he shall be blessed in the country. He shall be blessed when he comes in, and he shall be blessed when he goes out. I pray that You, LORD, will command Your blessing on him in his storehouses and in all to which he sets his hand.

DEUTERONOMY 28:2–3, 6, 8

———— ■ ————

I pray that my son will give, and it will be given to him: good measure, pressed down, shaken together, and running over will be put into his bosom. For with the same measure that he uses, it will be measured back to him.

LUKE 6:38

I pray that because freely my son has received, freely he will give.

MATTHEW 10:8

———— ■ ————

I pray that on the first day of the week my son will lay something aside, storing up as he may prosper, so that there be no collections when it is time to give.

1 CORINTHIANS 16:2

———— ■ ————

I pray that my son will bring all his tithes into the storehouse, that there may be food in God's house. And that he will try You, God, in this and see if You will not open for him the windows of heaven and pour out for him such blessing that there will not be room enough to receive it.

MALACHI 3:10

———— ■ ————

I pray that my son realizes that if he sows sparingly he will also reap sparingly, and if

he sows bountifully he will also reap
bountifully. I pray that he will give as he
purposes in his heart, not grudgingly or of
necessity; for You, God, love a cheerful giver.
And You are able to make all grace abound
toward him, that my son, always having all
sufficiency in all things, may have an
abundance for every good work.

2 CORINTHIANS 9:6–8

———— ■ ————

I pray that my son will remember that
everyone who has left houses or brothers
or sisters or father or mother or daughter
or children or lands, for Your name's sake,
Lord, shall receive a hundredfold, and inherit
eternal life. I pray also that he will remember
that many who are first will be last, and the
last first.

MATTHEW 19:29–30

———— ■ ————

I pray that this Book of the Law shall not
depart from my son's mouth, but he shall
meditate in it day and night, that he may

observe to do according to all that is written
in it. For then he will make his way
prosperous, and then he will have good
success.

JOSHUA 1:8

———— ■ ————

I pray, God, that You will give wisdom and
knowledge and joy to my son who is good
in Your sight; but to the sinner You will give
the work of gathering and collecting, that
he may give to my son who is good before
You.

ECCLESIASTES 2:26

———— ■ ————

I pray that my son leaves an inheritance to
his children's children.

PROVERBS 13:22

———— ■ ————

I pray that my son does not worry about
his life, saying, "What shall I eat?" or "What
shall I drink?" or "What shall I put on?" For

You, his heavenly Father, know that he needs all these things. But I pray that he will seek first Your kingdom, God, and Your righteousness, and all these things shall be added to him. I also pray that he does not worry about tomorrow, for tomorrow will worry about its own things.

MATTHEW 6:25, 31–34

■

I pray that You, God, shall supply all my son's needs according to Your riches in glory by Christ Jesus.

PHILIPPIANS 4:19

19

FORGIVENESS

Lord God, for reasons known to You, my son needs Your forgiveness. Because I sense that and know that he has need of Your forgiveness I come to You today, praying Your very words back to You in order that he might be forgiven. Bless now the very words from Your mouth on my son's behalf. Thank You now in Jesus' name. Amen.

God, in accordance with Your Word . . .

I pray that as far as the east is from the west, so far have You, God, removed my son's transgressions from him.

PSALM 103:12

———— ■ ————

I pray that it is You who blots out my son's transgressions for Your own sake and that You will not remember his sins.

ISAIAH 43:25

I pray that my son will return to You, LORD,
and that You will have mercy on him; and
to his God, for You will abundantly pardon.

ISAIAH 55:7

■

I pray that You, God, will cleanse my son
from all his iniquity by which he has sinned
against You, and that You will pardon all his
iniquities by which he has sinned and by
which he has transgressed against You.

JEREMIAH 33:8

■

I pray that my son's transgressions are
forgiven and his sin is covered.

PSALM 32:1

■

I pray that whenever my son stands praying,
if he has anything against anyone that he
will forgive them, so that You, his Father in
heaven, may also forgive him of his
trespasses.

MARK 11:25

I pray that my son will bear with others, and forgive others, if he has a complaint against any others; even as Christ forgave him, so he also must do.

COLOSSIANS 3:13

————— ■ —————

I pray that my son will walk by faith and not by sight.

2 CORINTHIANS 5:7

————— ■ —————

I pray that if my son confesses his sins, that You, God, are faithful and just to forgive his sins and to cleanse him from all unrighteousness.

1 JOHN 1:9

————— ■ —————

I pray that if my son sins, he has an Advocate with You, the Father, Jesus Christ the righteous.

1 JOHN 2:1

I pray that in You, Jesus, my son has redemption through Your blood, the forgiveness of his sins, according to the riches of God's grace which He made to abound toward him in all wisdom and prudence, having made known to him the mystery of His will, according to His good pleasure which He purposed in Himself.

EPHESIANS 1:7–9

20

GODLY LIFE

Lord Jesus, my Lord and my Savior, more than anything else I desire that my wonderful son will live a godly life in Your sight. Your words are my prayers to You on his behalf. Please honor them by keeping my son in the center of Your will in all that he does. Thank You for all that You do and especially for honoring this my prayer. Amen.

**God, in accordance
with Your Word . . .**

I pray that if my son lives, he lives to You, Lord; and if he dies, he dies to You, Lord. Therefore, whether he lives or dies, he is Yours, Lord.

ROMANS 14:8

━━━━━ ■ ━━━━━

I pray that what the law could not do in my son in that it was weak through the flesh, You, God, did by sending Your own Son in

the likeness of sinful flesh, on account of
sin: You condemned sin in my son, that the
righteous requirement of the law might be
fulfilled in him who does not walk according
to the flesh but according to the Spirit.

ROMANS 8:3–4

———— ■ ————

I pray that my son does not present his
members as instruments of unrighteousness
to sin, but presents himself to You, God, as
being alive from the dead, and his members
as instruments of righteousness to You. For
sin shall not have dominion over him, for
he is not under law but under grace.

ROMANS 6:13–14

———— ■ ————

I pray that my son will not be conformed
to this world, but that he will be transformed
by the renewing of his mind, that he may
prove what is that good and acceptable and
perfect will of God.

ROMANS 12:2

I pray that if my son believes on You, Jesus, who justifies the ungodly, his faith is accounted for righteousness.

ROMANS 4:5

———————— ■ ————————

I pray that my son will present his body as a living sacrifice, holy, acceptable to You, God.

ROMANS 12:1

———————— ■ ————————

I pray that my son will not think of himself more highly than he ought to think, but will think soberly, as You, God, have dealt to him a measure of faith.

ROMANS 12:3

———————— ■ ————————

I pray that because You, Christ, are in my son, his body is dead because of sin, but the Spirit is life because of righteousness.

ROMANS 8:10

I pray that my son whom You, God,
predestined, You also called; he whom You
called, You also justified; and he whom You
justified, You also glorified.

ROMANS 8:30

———— ■ ————

I pray that because my son is in You, Christ,
he is a new creation; old things have passed
away; behold, all things have become new.

2 CORINTHIANS 5:17

———— ■ ————

I pray that You, God, made Jesus who
knew no sin to be sin for my son, that he
might become the righteousness of You
in Him.

2 CORINTHIANS 5:21

———— ■ ————

I pray that You, God, are able to make all
grace abound toward my son, that he, always
having all sufficiency in all things, may have
an abundance for every good work.

2 CORINTHIANS 9:8

I pray that my son will remain in the same calling in which he was called.

1 CORINTHIANS 7:20

———— ■ ————

I pray that if my son glories, he will glory in You, Lord.

1 CORINTHIANS 1:31

———— ■ ————

I pray that my son will not let sin reign in his mortal body, that he should obey it in its lusts.

ROMANS 6:12

———— ■ ————

I pray that my son has been set free from sin and has become a slave of God.

ROMANS 6:22

———— ■ ————

I pray that my son will be renewed in the spirit of his mind, and that he will put on

his new self which was created according
to You, God, in true righteousness and
holiness.

EPHESIANS 4:23–24

■

I pray that it is good for my son to draw
near to You, God; to put his trust in the Lord
God, that he may declare all Your works.

PSALM 73:28

■

I pray that my son will delight himself in
You, LORD, and that You shall give him the
desires of his heart.

PSALM 37:4

■

I pray that You, God, will satisfy my son's
mouth with good things, so that his youth
is renewed like the eagle's.

PSALM 103:5

I pray that You, God, are a companion to my son who fears You and who keeps Your precepts.

PSALM 119:63

I pray that my son, who walks in the law of the LORD, will be blessed.

PSALM 119:1

I pray that my son's ways are directed to keep Your statutes, God.

PSALM 119:5

I pray that my son will cleanse his way by taking heed according to Your word, God.

PSALM 119:9

I pray that with my son's whole heart he has sought You, God. Let him not wander from Your commandments.

PSALM 119:10

I pray that my son has hidden Your word
in his heart, God, that he might not sin
against You.

PSALM 119:11

———— ■ ————

I pray that my son will delight himself in
Your statutes, God, and that he will not forget
Your word.

PSALM 119:16

———— ■ ————

I pray that You, God, will open my son's eyes,
that he may see wondrous things from Your
law.

PSALM 119:18

———— ■ ————

I pray that my son has declared his ways
and that You, God, have answered him and
that You will teach him Your statutes.

PSALM 119:26

I pray, God, that Your testimonies also are
my son's delight and his counselors.

PSALM 119:24

■

I pray that You, God, will make my son
understand the way of Your precepts; so shall
he meditate on Your wondrous works.

PSALM 119:27

■

I pray that my son has chosen the way of
truth and that Your judgments he has laid
before him. I pray that he will cling to Your
testimonies, LORD, and that he will not be
put to shame.

PSALM 119:30–31

■

I pray, God, that You will make my son walk
in the path of Your commandments and that
he will delight in it.

PSALM 119:35

I pray that my son will incline his heart to Your testimonies, God, and not to covetousness. I pray that he will turn away his eyes from looking at worthless things and that You will revive him in Your way.

PSALM 119:36–37

■

I pray that You, God, will remember the word to my son, Your servant, upon which You have caused him to hope.

PSALM 119:49

■

I pray that You, God, will be merciful to my son according to Your word.

PSALM 119:58

■

I pray, O God, that my son has thought about his ways, and has turned his feet to Your testimonies. I pray that he has made haste, and has not delayed to keep Your commandments.

PSALM 119:59–60

I pray that You, God, will teach my son good
judgment and knowledge, for he believes
Your commandments.

PSALM 119:66

———— ■ ————

I pray, God, that Your hands have made my
son and fashioned him. Give him
understanding that he may learn Your
commandments.

PSALM 119:73

———— ■ ————

I pray, God, that You will let Your merciful
kindness be for my son's comfort.

PSALM 119:76

———— ■ ————

I pray, God, that You will let my son's heart
be blameless regarding Your statutes, that
he may not be ashamed.

PSALM 119:80

I pray, Lord God, that my son will never forget Your precepts, for by them You have given him life.

PSALM 119:93

———— ■ ————

I pray that You, God, are my son's hiding place and his shield and that his hope is in Your word.

PSALM 119:114

———— ■ ————

I pray that You, God, will give my son understanding that he may know Your testimonies.

PSALM 119:125

———— ■ ————

I pray that my son shall love You, the Lord his God, with all his heart, with all his soul, with all his mind, and with all his strength and that he shall love his neighbor as himself.

MARK 12:30–31

I pray that my son's steps are directed by
Your word, God, and that You let no iniquity
have dominion over him.

PSALM 119:133

———— ■ ————

I pray that Your word, O God, is a lamp to
my son's feet and a light to his path.

PSALM 119:105

———— ■ ————

I pray that You, Jesus, are always at my son's
right hand, that he may not be shaken.

ACTS 2:25

———— ■ ————

I pray that my son may gain You, Christ, and
be found in You, not having his own
righteousness, which is from the law, but that
which is through faith in You, the
righteousness which is from God by faith;
that he may know You and the power of

Your resurrection, and the fellowship of Your
sufferings, being conformed to Your death.

PHILIPPIANS 3:8–10

———— ■ ————

I pray that if my son confesses his sins, that
You, God, are faithful and just to forgive his
sins and to cleanse him from all
unrighteousness.

1 JOHN 1:9

———— ■ ————

I pray that the work of my son's
righteousness will be peace, and the effect
of his righteousness, quietness and assurance
forever.

ISAIAH 32:17

———— ■ ————

I pray that blessed is my son who walks not
in the counsel of the ungodly, nor stands
in the path of sinners, nor sits in the seat
of the scornful. But his delight is in the law
of the LORD, and in Your law he meditates

day and night. I pray that he shall be like a tree planted by the rivers of water, that brings forth its fruit in its season, whose leaf also shall not wither; and whatever he does shall prosper.

PSALM 1:1–3

———— ■ ————

I pray that my son shall know the truth and the truth shall make him free.

JOHN 8:32

———— ■ ————

I pray that my son takes up Your whole armor, God, that he may be able to withstand in the evil day, and having done all, to stand. I pray that he will gird his waist with truth, that he will put on the breastplate of righteousness, and will shod his feet with the preparation of the gospel of peace; and above all, take the shield of faith with which he will be able to quench all the fiery darts of the wicked one. I pray that he will take the helmet of salvation, and the sword of the Spirit, which is the word of God; praying

always with all prayer and supplication in
the Spirit, being watchful to this end with
all perseverance and supplication for all the
saints.

EPHESIANS 6:13–18

———— ■ ————

I pray that my son will be diligent to present
himself approved to You, God, a worker who
does not need to be ashamed, rightly
dividing the word of truth.

2 TIMOTHY 2:15

———— ■ ————

I pray that my son will not be deceived, for
You, God, are not mocked; for whatever he
sows, that he will also reap.

GALATIANS 6:7

———— ■ ————

I pray that my son always remembers that
all Scripture is given by inspiration of You,
God, and is profitable for doctrine, for
reproof, for correction, for instruction in

righteousness, that the man of God may
be complete, thoroughly equipped for every
good work.

2 TIMOTHY 3:16–17

———— ■ ————

I pray that no one deceives my son with
empty words.

EPHESIANS 5:6

———— ■ ————

I pray that my son will be a doer of the word,
and not a hearer only.

JAMES 1:22

21

GOD'S LOVE

Lord God, I pray Your words to You as my way to ask You to love my son in a very special way. Help him, Lord, to experience Your love through Your word and through other ways as well. Thank You, Father, in Jesus' name. Amen.

God, in accordance with Your Word . . .

I pray that my son knows that love is not that he loved You, God, but that You loved him and sent Your Son to be the propitiation for his sins.

1 JOHN 4:10

———— ■ ————

I pray that my son loves You, God, because You first loved him.

1 JOHN 4:19

I pray that You, Christ, may dwell in my son's heart through faith and that he, being rooted and grounded in love, may be able to comprehend with all the saints what is the width and length and depth and height—to know Your love which passes knowledge; that he may be filled with all the fullness of God.

EPHESIANS 3:17–19

I pray that my son never forgets that You, God, demonstrated Your own love toward him, in that while he was still a sinner, Christ died for him.

ROMANS 5:8

I pray that neither death nor life, nor angels nor principalities nor powers, nor things present nor things to come, nor height nor depth, nor any other created thing, shall be able to separate my son from the love of You, God, which is in Christ Jesus, his Lord.

ROMANS 8:38–39

I pray that You, God, so loved my son that You gave Your only begotten Son, that my son who believes in Him should not perish but have everlasting life.

JOHN 3:16

———————— ■ ————————

I pray that my son has Your commandments, Jesus, and keeps them and loves You. And because he loves You he will be loved by God, and You will love him and manifest Yourself to him.

JOHN 14:21

———————— ■ ————————

I pray that my son knows that You, God, have loved him with an everlasting love and with lovingkindness You have drawn him.

JEREMIAH 31:3

———————— ■ ————————

I pray that my son realizes that You, God, will rejoice over him with gladness. That You will quiet him with Your love and that You will rejoice over him with singing.

ZEPHANIAH 3:17

22

GOD'S WORD

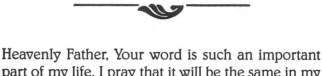

Heavenly Father, Your word is such an important part of my life. I pray that it will be the same in my son's life and that Your word will be living and sharper than any two-edged sword in his life. I'm praying Your word for Your word to be important to him. Thank You, Father, in Jesus' name, for hearing and answering my prayers for my son. Amen.

God, in accordance
with Your Word . . .

I pray that my son has been born again, not of corruptible seed but incorruptible, through Your word, God, which lives and abides forever.

1 PETER 1:23

■

I pray that my son never forgets that the word of the Lord endures forever.

1 PETER 1:25

I pray, God, that in my son's life Your word
is living and powerful, and sharper than any
two-edged sword, piercing even to the
division of his soul and spirit, and of his
joints and marrow, and that it is a discerner
of the thoughts and intents of his heart.

HEBREWS 4:12

I pray that my son puts into practice the fact
that he shall not live by bread alone, but
by every word that proceeds from the mouth
of God.

MATTHEW 4:4

I pray that my son will always understand
and apply the fact that all Scripture is given
by Your inspiration, God, and is profitable
for doctrine, for reproof, for correction, for
instruction in righteousness, that he may be
complete, thoroughly equipped for every
good work.

2 TIMOTHY 3:16–17

I pray that my son knows that he has been given exceedingly great and precious promises, that through these he may be a partaker of the divine nature, having escaped the corruption that is in the world through lust.

2 PETER 1:4

———— ■ ————

I pray that my son understands the significance of the fact that until heaven and earth pass away, one jot or one tittle will by no means pass from the law till all is fulfilled.

MATTHEW 5:18

———— ■ ————

I pray that my son takes to heart the fact that heaven and earth will pass away, but Your words, Jesus, will by no means pass away.

MARK 13:31

I pray that my son always remembers that heaven and earth will pass away, but Jesus' words will by no means pass away.

MATTHEW 24:35

———— ■ ————

I pray that if my son will abide in Your word, Jesus, he is Your disciple indeed. And if he does that he shall know the truth, and the truth shall make him free.

JOHN 8:31–32

———— ■ ————

I pray that my son's walk with You, Lord, will be so close that his ears shall hear a word behind him, saying, "This is the way, walk in it."

ISAIAH 30:21

———— ■ ————

I pray that my son realizes the significance of the fact that You, God, said, "So shall My word be that goes forth from My mouth; it shall not return to Me void."

ISAIAH 55:11

I pray that You, O God, will instruct my son
and teach him in the way he should go and
that You will guide him with Your eye.

PSALM 32:8

———— ■ ————

I pray that my son will not be like the horse
or like the mule, which have no
understanding and which must be harnessed
with bit and bridle, else they will not come
near you.

PSALM 32:9

———— ■ ————

I pray, O God, that my son will take Your
testimonies as a heritage forever, for they
are the rejoicing of his heart.

PSALM 119:111

———— ■ ————

I pray that my son is Your servant, O God,
and that You will give him understanding
that he may know Your testimonies.

PSALM 119:125

I pray that my son will give attention to Your words, O God, that he will incline his ear to Your sayings. Do not let them depart from his eyes and keep them in the midst of his heart, for they are life to him when he finds them and health to his flesh.

PROVERBS 4:20–22

I pray, God, that my son will know that every word of God is pure and that You are a shield to those who put their trust in You. I pray that he will not add to Your words, lest You rebuke him, and he be found a liar.

PROVERBS 30:5–6

I pray, God, that my son will not let Your Book of the Law depart from his mouth, but he shall meditate in it day and night, that he may observe to do according to all that is written in it. For then he will make his way prosperous, and then he will have good success.

JOSHUA 1:8

23
GRIEF / HURTING

God, You know the hurt in my son's life. And You already know other hurts that are yet to come to him. By and through Your word I pray that You will console my son in a very special way. Wipe away his tears and bring joy back into his life. I pray Your own words for those results. Please hear and honor them in Jesus' name. Amen.

**God, in accordance
with Your Word . . .**

I pray that You, God, will console my son who mourns and give him beauty for ashes, the oil of joy for mourning, the garment of praise for the spirit of heaviness so that he may be called a tree of righteousness.

ISAIAH 61:3

I pray, O God, that You will comfort my son in all his tribulations, that he may be able

to comfort those who are in any trouble,
with the comfort with which he himself is
comforted by You.

2 CORINTHIANS 1:4

———— ■ ————

I pray that my son is blessed when he
mourns for he shall be comforted.

MATTHEW 5:4

———— ■ ————

I pray that my son will not be ignorant
concerning those who have fallen asleep,
lest he sorrow as others who have no hope.

1 THESSALONIANS 4:13

———— ■ ————

I pray, O God, that You have comforted my
son and will have mercy on his affliction.

ISAIAH 49:13

———— ■ ————

I pray that when my son passes through the
waters, You, God, will be with him and

through the rivers, they shall not overflow
him. When he walks through the fire, he shall
not be burned, nor shall the flame scorch
him.

ISAIAH 43:2

■

I pray that the Lord Jesus Christ Himself and
You, God, who have loved my son and given
him everlasting consolation and good hope
by grace, will comfort his heart and establish
him in every good word and work.

2 THESSALONIANS 2:16–17

■

I pray that my son always remembers that
in You, Jesus, he does not have a High Priest
who cannot sympathize with his weaknesses,
but was in all points tempted as he is, yet
without sin. Let him therefore come boldly
to the throne of grace, that he may obtain
mercy and find grace to help in time of
need.

HEBREWS 4:15–16

I pray that though my son may walk through the valley of the shadow of death, he will fear no evil; for You, God, are with him and Your rod and Your staff, they comfort him.

PSALM 23:4

———— ■ ————

I pray that in this crucial time in my son's life he can say, "O Death, where is your sting? O Hades, where is your victory?"

1 CORINTHIANS 15:55

———— ■ ————

I pray that You, God, will wipe away every tear from my son's eyes and that there shall be no more death, nor sorrow, nor crying. I pray that there shall be no more pain, for the former things have passed away.

REVELATION 21:4

———— ■ ————

I pray that my son will fear not, for You, God, are with him. I pray that he will be

not dismayed, for You are his God. I pray
that You will strengthen him and help him
and that You will uphold him with Your
righteous right hand.

ISAIAH 41:10

———— ■ ————

I pray that my son shall obtain joy and
gladness and that sorrow and sighing shall
flee away.

ISAIAH 51:11

———— ■ ————

I pray that this is my son's comfort in his
affliction, that Your word, God, has given
him life.

PSALM 119:50

———— ■ ————

I pray that my son will cast all his cares upon
You, O God, for You care for him.

1 PETER 5:7

I pray that my son will walk by faith and
not by sight and that he is confident, yes,
well pleased rather to be absent from the
body and to be present with You, Lord.

2 CORINTHIANS 5:8

24

INHERITANCE

Lord God, in Your Son's name and through Your perfect word I pray that my son will be fully aware of and never forget the magnitude of the inheritance that awaits him. Give him a vision of that inheritance as even now I pray Your words for him. Thank You, God, in Jesus' name. Amen.

God, in accordance with Your Word . . .

I pray that whatever my son does, he will do it heartily, as to You, Lord, and not to men, knowing that from You he will receive the reward of the inheritance; for he serves the Lord Christ.

COLOSSIANS 3:23–24

■

I pray that my son has been given exceedingly great and precious promises,

that through these he may be a partaker of
the divine nature, having escaped the
corruption that is in the world through lust.

2 PETER 1:4

■

I pray that my son has an inheritance
incorruptible and undefiled and that does
not fade away, reserved in heaven for him.

1 PETER 1:4

■

I commend my son to You, God, and to the
word of Your grace, which is able to build
him up and give him an inheritance among
all those who are sanctified.

ACTS 20:32

■

I pray, God, that the Spirit Himself bears
witness with my spirit that my son is a child
of Yours and if a child, then an heir—an heir
of Yours and a joint heir with Christ, if indeed

he suffers with Him, that he may also be
glorified together with Him.

ROMANS 8:16–17

---------- ■ ----------

I pray that my son in You, Jesus, has obtained
an inheritance, being predestined according
to the purpose of Him who works all things
according to the counsel of His will, that
he who first trusted in You should be to the
praise of His glory. In You, Jesus, he also
trusted, after he heard the word of truth,
the gospel of his salvation; in whom also,
having believed, he was sealed with the Holy
Spirit of promise, who is the guarantee of
our inheritance until the redemption of the
purchased possession, to the praise of His
glory.

EPHESIANS 1:11–14

---------- ■ ----------

I pray, Lord, that my son is aware that eye
has not seen, nor ear heard, nor have

entered into his heart the things which You
have prepared for those who love You.

1 CORINTHIANS 2:9

———— ■ ————

I pray that my son always remembers that
in Your house, God, are many mansions and
if it were not so, Jesus would have told him.
Help him to remember that Jesus has gone
to prepare a place for him and if He goes
and prepares a place for him He will come
again and receive him to Himself, that where
He is, there he may be also.

JOHN 14:2–3

25

LONELY

Jesus, I pray to You concerning any feeling of being lonely that my son may be experiencing now or may experience in the future. As I pray Your words help him to remember that You said You would be with him always and that You are his constant companion. I pray Your very words to this end. In Your name I pray. Amen.

God, in accordance
with Your Word . . .

I pray that my son's conduct will be without covetousness, and that he will be content with such things as he has. For You, God, said, "I will never leave you nor forsake you."

HEBREWS 13:5

———— ■ ————

I pray that my son will fear not, for You, God, are with him. That he be not dismayed, for You are his God. I pray that You will strengthen him and that You will help him and that You will uphold him with Your righteous right hand.

ISAIAH 41:10

———— ■ ————

I pray that my son realizes that You, God, count the number of the stars and call them all by name. I pray that he remembers that great is his Lord and mighty in power and that Your understanding is infinite.

PSALM 147:4–5

———— ■ ————

I pray that my son remembers Jesus' promise to be with him always, even to the end of the age.

MATTHEW 28:20

———— ■ ————

I pray, Jesus, that my son remembers Your promise that You will not leave him as an orphan but that You will come to him.

JOHN 14:18

I pray, God, that neither death nor life, nor angels nor principalities nor powers, nor things present nor things to come, nor height nor depth, nor any other created thing, shall be able to separate my son from Your love, God, which is in Christ Jesus his Lord.

ROMANS 8:38–39

I pray that my son will be strong and of good courage and that he will not fear nor be afraid, for You, the LORD his God, You are the One who goes with him. I pray that You will not leave him nor forsake him.

DEUTERONOMY 31:6

I pray that though the mountains shall depart and the hills be removed, Your kindness, God, shall not depart from my son, nor shall Your covenant of peace be removed from him.

ISAIAH 54:10

I pray that if even I forsake my son, then
You, LORD, will take care of him.

PSALM 27:10

———— ■ ————

I pray, O God, that You are my son's refuge
and strength and a very present help in
trouble.

PSALM 46:1

26

LOVE

God, Your word tells us that You are love and that we must love others even as You have loved us. This is such an important matter that I want now to pray Your very words on this subject to You on my son's behalf. Honor Your words, Lord, as my prayers for my son. Thank You for the privilege of praying in Jesus' name. Amen.

God, in accordance with Your Word . . .

I pray that my son will love others, for love is of You, God.

1 JOHN 4:7

———— ■ ————

I pray that my son understands the true meaning of love and that though he speaks with the tongues of men and of angels, but has not love, he has become sounding brass

or a clanging cymbal. And though he has
the gift of prophecy, and understands all
mysteries and all knowledge, and though
he has all faith, so that he can remove
mountains, but has not love, he is nothing.
And though he bestows all his goods to feed
the poor, and though he gives his body to
be burned, but has not love, it profits him
nothing. I pray that he remembers that love
suffers long and is kind; love does not envy;
love does not parade itself, is not puffed up;
does not behave rudely, does not seek its
own, is not provoked, thinks no evil; does
not rejoice in iniquity, but rejoices in the
truth; bears all things, believes all things,
hopes all things, endures all things. Help him
to understand that love never fails. Help him
to abide in faith, hope, love, these three; but
the greatest of these is love.

1 CORINTHIANS 13:1–8, 13

I pray that my son understands that love is
not that he loved You, God, but that You
loved him and sent Your Son to be the
propitiation for his sins. And help him to

know that if You so loved him, he also ought
to love others.

1 JOHN 4:10–11

———————— ■ ————————

I pray that my son totally understands that
as You, God, loved Jesus, He also has loved
him and he is to abide in His love.

JOHN 15:9

———————— ■ ————————

I pray that if my son has Jesus'
commandments and keeps them, it is he
who loves Him. And my son who loves Jesus
will be loved by You, God, and Jesus will
love him and manifest Himself to him.

JOHN 14:21

———————— ■ ————————

I pray that You, God, will bring to my son's
mind that it is Jesus' commandment that he
love others just as He has loved him.

JOHN 15:12

I pray that my son shall love You, the Lord
his God, with all his heart, with all his soul,
with all his mind, and with all his strength
and that he shall love his neighbor as
himself.

MARK 12:30–31

———— ■ ————

I pray that my son has known and believed
the love that You, God, have for him and
that he who loves You must love his brother
also.

1 JOHN 4:16, 21

———— ■ ————

I pray, God, that You have loved my son with
an everlasting love and with lovingkindness
have drawn him to You.

JEREMIAH 31:3

———— ■ ————

I pray, Jesus, that my son will take heed to
the new commandment You gave to him
that he love others as You have loved him

and that by this he will know that he is Your
disciple, if he has love for others.

JOHN 13:34–35

———— ■ ————

I pray that You, God, love my son, because
he has loved Jesus, and has believed that
He came forth from You.

JOHN 16:27

———— ■ ————

I pray that my son will realize that You, God,
demonstrated Your own love toward him
in that while he was still a sinner, Christ died
for him.

ROMANS 5:8

———— ■ ————

I pray that You, God, so loved my son that
You gave Your only begotten Son, that he
who believes in Him should not perish but
have everlasting life.

JOHN 3:16

I pray that neither death nor life, nor angels nor principalities nor powers, nor things present nor things to come, nor height nor depth, nor any other created thing, shall be able to separate my son from Your love, God, which is in Christ Jesus his Lord.

ROMANS 8:38–39

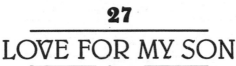

27
LOVE FOR MY SON

Lord, I pray these Your words for my son. Honor my prayers by honoring Your own words. I praise You and pray to You in Jesus' name. Amen.

God, in accordance with Your Word . . .

I pray that while my son and I have not seen You, God, at any time, if we love one another, You abide in us, and Your love has been perfected in us.

1 JOHN 4:12

———— ■ ————

I pray, Jesus, that my son and I will follow Your commandment that we love one another as You have loved us.

JOHN 15:12

I pray that if You, God, so loved my son and me, we also ought to love one another.

1 JOHN 4:11

———— ■ ————

I pray, Lord Jesus, that by this my son and I know love, because You laid down Your life for us. And we also ought to lay down our lives for each other.

1 JOHN 3:16

———— ■ ————

I pray, Lord God, that my son and I will love one another, for love is of You; and everyone who loves is born of You and knows You. But if we do not love we do not know You, for You are love.

1 JOHN 4:7–8

———— ■ ————

I pray, Jesus, that my son and I will follow Your command that we love one another.

JOHN 15:17

I pray, Lord Jesus, that my son and I always
remember that when we were still without
strength, in due time You died for us.

ROMANS 5:6

———— ■ ————

I pray that my son and I will always
understand the significance of the question,
"Can two walk together, unless they are
agreed?"

AMOS 3:3

28

NEEDS

Lord, You and You alone know all of my son's needs. I desire now to spend time with You praying Your word over his needs and to ask You to bless the praying of Your word and to honor the praying of Your word by meeting my son's needs as only You can do. I pray Your words now in Jesus' name. Amen.

God, in accordance
with Your Word . . .

I pray that my son will delight himself also in You, LORD, and that You will give him the desires of his heart.

PSALM 37:4

— ■ —

I pray that You, God, will open Your hand and satisfy the desire of my son.

PSALM 145:16

I pray that You, LORD, will guide my son continually.

ISAIAH 58:11

———— ■ ————

I pray that my son will not spend wages for what does not satisfy and that he will listen carefully to You, God, and will let his soul delight itself in abundance.

ISAIAH 55:2

———— ■ ————

I pray that whatever things my son asks in prayer, believing, he will receive.

MATTHEW 21:22

———— ■ ————

I pray, Lord Jesus, that if my son abides in You and Your words abide in him, he will ask what he desires, and it shall be done for him.

JOHN 15:7

I pray, Jesus, that if my son asks anything
in Your name, You will do it.

JOHN 14:14

———— ■ ————

I pray that my son will ask in Your name,
Jesus, and he will receive, that his joy may
be full.

JOHN 16:24

———— ■ ————

I pray that my son shall know the truth and
the truth shall make him free.

JOHN 8:32

———— ■ ————

I pray that You, the God and Father of our
Lord Jesus Christ, have blessed my son with
every spiritual blessing in the heavenly
places in Christ.

EPHESIANS 1:3

I pray that my son can do all things through
Christ who strengthens him.

PHILIPPIANS 4:13

———— ■ ————

I pray that You, my God, shall supply all my
son's needs according to Your riches in glory
by Christ Jesus.

PHILIPPIANS 4:19

———— ■ ————

I pray that if my son's heart does not
condemn him, he has confidence toward
You, God. And whatever he asks he receives
from You, because he keeps Your
commandments and does those things that
are pleasing in Your sight.

1 JOHN 3:21–22

29

OBEDIENCE

God, You have said that obedience is more important to You than is sacrifice. Because I believe that You meant what You said I now pray back to You Your powerful words. God, in Jesus' name I ask You to help my son be obedient to You in every way and in every situation. Having asked You for it in Jesus' name, I believe that it will happen and I thank You in His name. Amen.

God, in accordance with Your Word . . .

I pray that my son recognizes the fact that You, God, have set before him today a blessing and a curse: the blessing, if he obeys the commandments of the LORD his God which You have commanded him today; and the curse, if he does not obey the commandments of the LORD his God, but turns aside from the way which You

command him today, to go after other gods
which he has not known.

DEUTERONOMY 11:26–28

———— ■ ————

I pray that my son never forgets that to obey
is better than sacrifice.

1 SAMUEL 15:22

———— ■ ————

I pray that my son will heed Your
commandments, O God, so that his peace
will be like a river and his righteousness like
the waves of the sea.

ISAIAH 48:18

———— ■ ————

I pray, O God, that my son will obey Your
voice, and You will be his God, and he shall
be Your child. And that he will walk in all
the ways that You have commanded him,
that it may be well with him.

JEREMIAH 7:23

I pray, Lord Jesus, that my son loves You
and keeps Your commandments.

JOHN 14:15

———— ■ ————

I pray, God, that my son knows that he ought
to obey You rather than men.

ACTS 5:29

———— ■ ————

I pray, Jesus, that my son will always keep
Your commandments.

1 JOHN 2:3

———— ■ ————

I pray that my son will learn Your statutes,
O God, and be careful to observe them. I
pray that he will be careful to do as You,
the LORD his God, have commanded him and
that he shall not turn aside to the right hand
or to the left. I pray that he will walk in all
the ways which You have commanded him,
that he may live and that it may be well with
him, and that you may prolong his days.

DEUTERONOMY 5:1, 32–33

I pray that my son will walk in Your ways, God, to keep Your statutes and Your commandments, and that You will lengthen his days.

1 KINGS 3:14

———— ■ ————

I pray that You, God, will teach my son to do Your will, for You are his God.

PSALM 143:10

———— ■ ————

I pray that whatever my son does, he does it heartily, as to the Lord and not to men.

COLOSSIANS 3:23

30

PATIENCE

Lord Jesus, patience is so important but so elusive.
I pray to You now what You have already declared
in Your word and I ask You to honor it in my son's
life. Bless now the praying of Your word. Amen.

God, in accordance
with Your Word . . .

I pray that whatever things were written for
my son's learning, that he through the
patience and comfort of the Scriptures might
have hope. Now may You, the God of
patience and comfort, grant my son to be
like-minded toward others, according to
Christ Jesus.

ROMANS 15:4–5

———————— ■ ————————

I pray that my son will glory in tribulations,
knowing that tribulation produces

perseverance; and perseverance, character;
and character, hope.

ROMANS 5:3–4

———— ■ ————

I pray that my son will rest in You, LORD,
and that he will wait patiently for You. I pray
that he does not fret because of him who
prospers in his way, or because of the man
who brings wicked schemes to pass. I pray
that he will cease from anger, and forsake
wrath and that he does not fret—it only
causes harm.

PSALM 37:7–8

———— ■ ————

I pray that my son will wait patiently for You,
LORD, and that You will incline Yourself to
him and hear his cry.

PSALM 40:1

———— ■ ————

I pray that my son does not cast away his
confidence, which has great reward. For he

has need of endurance, so that after he has done Your will, God, he may receive his promise.

HEBREWS 10:35–36

———— ■ ————

I pray that since my son is surrounded by so great a cloud of witnesses, let him lay aside every weight, and the sin which so easily ensnares him, and let him run with endurance the race that is set before him.

HEBREWS 12:1

———— ■ ————

I pray that my son will not hasten in his spirit to be angry, for anger rests in the bosom of fools.

ECCLESIASTES 7:9

———— ■ ————

I pray that my son will imitate those who through faith and patience inherit the promises.

HEBREWS 6:12

I pray that the fruit of the Spirit in my son
is love, joy, peace, longsuffering, kindness,
goodness, faithfulness, gentleness, and self-
control.

GALATIANS 5:22–23

■

I pray that my son will wait on You, LORD,
and that he shall renew his strength. I pray
that he shall mount up with wings like
eagles, he shall run and not be weary, and
that he shall walk and not faint.

ISAIAH 40:31

■

I pray that my son will wait on You, LORD,
and that he will be of good courage. I also
pray that You will strengthen his heart and
that he will wait on You.

PSALM 27:14

■

I pray that my son will hope and wait quietly
for Your salvation, O LORD.

LAMENTATIONS 3:26

I pray that my son will hope for what he does not see and eagerly wait for it with perseverance.

ROMANS 8:25

———— ■ ————

I pray that my son understands that the testing of his faith produces patience and that he should let patience have its perfect work, that he may be perfect and complete, lacking nothing.

JAMES 1:3–4

———— ■ ————

I pray that my son will be patient until Your coming, Lord. I pray that he will see how the farmer waits for the precious fruit of the earth, waiting patiently for it until it receives the early and latter rain and that he also will be patient, for Your coming is near.

JAMES 5:7–8

31

PEACE

Heavenly Father, just as Your word says, I pray perfect peace for my son. There is no process that I know of that is more important to his having peace than to pray Your words of promised peace to him. It is Your words that I pray in Jesus' name and I thank You for hearing and answering these my prayers. Amen.

God, in accordance
with Your Word . . .

I pray, God, that You will keep my son in perfect peace, whose mind is stayed on You, because he trusts in You.

ISAIAH 26:3

———— ■ ————

I pray that Your kindness, God, shall not depart from my son, nor shall Your covenant of peace be removed from him.

ISAIAH 54:10

I pray that my son will lie down in peace, and sleep; for You alone, O LORD, make him dwell in safety.

PSALM 4:8

———— ■ ————

I pray, O LORD, that You will give strength to my son and that You will bless him with peace.

PSALM 29:11

———— ■ ————

I pray that You, Jesus, have left Your peace with my son. I pray that his heart will not be troubled, neither will he be afraid.

JOHN 14:27

———— ■ ————

I pray that my son who has been justified by faith, will have peace with You, God, through his Lord Jesus Christ.

ROMANS 5:1

I pray that Jesus Himself is my son's peace.

EPHESIANS 2:14

———————— ■ ————————

I pray that my son will be anxious for nothing, but in everything by prayer and supplication, with thanksgiving, will let his requests be made known to You, God; and Your peace which surpasses all understanding, will guard his heart and mind through Christ Jesus.

PHILIPPIANS 4:6–7

———————— ■ ————————

I pray, God, that the peace of God rules in my son's heart.

COLOSSIANS 3:15

32

POWER

Lord God, my son is in need of Your power. That power comes only through Your word and that is what I pray to You today. Honor the praying of Your word and bring Your power into the life of my son. It is in the powerful name of Jesus that I offer up Your words to You in prayer for my son. Thank You for hearing and answering each of these prayers. Amen.

God, in accordance with Your Word . . .

I pray that in all things my son is more than a conqueror through Jesus who loved him.

ROMANS 8:37

I pray that my son can do all things through Christ who strengthens him.

PHILIPPIANS 4:13

I pray that my son will take pleasure in infirmities, in reproaches, in needs, in persecutions, in distresses, for Christ's sake. For when he is weak, then he is strong.

2 CORINTHIANS 12:10

I pray, Jesus, that whatever my son asks in Your name that You will do, that the Father may be glorified in the Son.

JOHN 14:13

I pray that You, God, are able to make all grace abound toward my son, that he, always having all sufficiency in all things, may have an abundance for every good work.

2 CORINTHIANS 9:8

I pray, Jesus, that Your grace is sufficient for my son, for Your strength is made perfect in weakness.

2 CORINTHIANS 12:9

I pray that my son will see the exceeding greatness of Your power, God, toward him who believes, according to the working of Your mighty power.

EPHESIANS 1:19

■

I pray, O God, that You are able to do exceedingly abundantly above all that my son asks or thinks, according to the power that works in him.

EPHESIANS 3:20

33

PRAISE

Heavenly Father, we were created to praise You. Through the praying of Your word I petition You to put into my son's heart a consistent desire to praise You at all times. These words of Yours are my prayers in Jesus' name. Amen.

God, in accordance with Your Word . . .

I pray, LORD God, that my son will sing praises to You and that he will declare Your deeds among the people.

PSALM 9:11

■

I pray that every day my son will bless You, God, and will praise Your name forever and ever.

PSALM 145:2

I pray that my son will sing praises to You, LORD, as long as he lives.

PSALM 104:33

———— ■ ————

I pray that my son will know that great is the LORD, and greatly to be praised and that Your greatness is unsearchable.

PSALM 145:3

———— ■ ————

I pray that my son's tongue shall speak of Your righteousness, Lord, and of Your praise all the day long.

PSALM 35:28

———— ■ ————

I pray that my son will give You thanks, O Lord God Almighty, the One who is and who was and who is to come, because You have taken Your great power and reigned.

REVELATION 11:17

I pray, O Lord, that You will open my son's
lips and his mouth shall show forth Your
praise.

PSALM 51:15

———— ∎ ————

I pray, O LORD, that my son will praise You.

ISAIAH 12:1

———— ∎ ————

I pray that my son will hope continually, O
God, and will praise You yet more and more.

PSALM 71:14

———— ∎ ————

I pray, God, that my son will enter into Your
gates with thanksgiving and into Your courts
with praise.

PSALM 100:4

———— ∎ ————

I pray that my son always remembers that
You, LORD, are great and greatly to be praised.

1 CHRONICLES 16:25

I pray that You, LORD, are my son's strength
and song and that You have become his
salvation; that You are his God, and that he
will praise You.

EXODUS 15:2

■

I pray that my son will proclaim the name
of the LORD and ascribe greatness to You
his God.

DEUTERONOMY 32:3

■

I pray that my son will proclaim, "The LORD
lives! Blessed be my Rock! Let God be
exalted, the Rock of my salvation!"

2 SAMUEL 22:47

■

I pray that my son will bless You, LORD, at
all times and that Your praise shall
continually be in his mouth.

PSALM 34:1

I pray, God, that You have put a new song
in my son's mouth—Praise to his God.

PSALM 40:3

———————— ■ ————————

I pray that my son realizes that great is the
LORD and greatly to be praised.

PSALM 48:1

———————— ■ ————————

I pray that my son prays, "Blessed be the
Lord, who daily loads me with benefits."

PSALM 68:19

———————— ■ ————————

I pray that my son will give thanks to You,
LORD, for You are good! For Your mercy
endures forever.

PSALM 106:1

———————— ■ ————————

I pray that my son will praise You, God, for
he is fearfully and wonderfully made.

Marvelous are Your works, and that his soul
knows very well.

PSALM 139:14

———— ■ ————

I pray that my son's mouth shall speak the
praise of You, God.

PSALM 145:21

———— ■ ————

I pray that my son will praise You, LORD!

PSALM 146:1

———— ■ ————

I pray that my son will praise You, God, for
Your mighty acts and that he will praise You
according to Your excellent greatness.

PSALM 150:2

———— ■ ————

I pray that You will let my son's soul live,
O God, and it shall praise You.

PSALM 119:175

I pray that my son will continually offer the sacrifice of praise to You, God, that is, the fruit of his lips, giving thanks to Your name.

HEBREWS 13:15

34

PROTECTION

Lord God, honor the prayers I lift up to You for my son's protection. They are Your words straight from Your Bible. Protect him at all times through the praying of Your word in Jesus' name. Amen.

**God, in accordance
with Your Word . . .**

I pray that my son's LORD God, who goes before him, will fight for him.

DEUTERONOMY 1:30

———— ■ ————

I pray that if my son will indeed obey Your voice, God, and do all that You speak, then You will be an enemy to his enemies and an adversary to his adversaries.

EXODUS 23:22

I pray that no weapon formed against my son shall prosper and every tongue which rises against him in judgment, You, God, shall condemn.

ISAIAH 54:17

———— ■ ————

I pray that Jesus has given my son the authority to trample on serpents and scorpions, and over all the power of the enemy, and nothing shall by any means hurt him.

LUKE 10:19

———— ■ ————

I pray that You, Lord, are faithful, who will establish my son and guard him from the evil one.

2 THESSALONIANS 3:3

———— ■ ————

I pray that if God is for my son, who can be against him?

ROMANS 8:31

35

REBELLIOUS

Lord God, through the power of Your word I pray that no spirit of rebellion will ever enter into my son. Through the praying of Your word keep him free from any rebellious spirit or attitude. I pray to You and I thank You in Jesus' precious name. Amen.

God, in accordance
with Your Word . . .

I pray that my son, by doing good, may put to silence the ignorance of foolish men.

1 PETER 2:15

———— ■ ————

I pray that my son will gird up the loins of his mind, be sober, and rest his hope fully upon the grace that is to be brought to him at the revelation of Jesus Christ; as an obedient child, not conforming himself to

the former lusts, as in his ignorance; but as
You, God, who called him is holy, he also
is to be holy in all his conduct.

1 PETER 1:13–15

———— ■ ————

I pray that my son is aware that rebellion
is as the sin of witchcraft.

1 SAMUEL 15:23

———— ■ ————

I pray that my son will obey those who rule
over him, and be submissive, for they watch
out for his soul, as those who must give
account.

HEBREWS 13:17

———— ■ ————

I pray, God, that my son knows that You
resist the proud, but give grace to the
humble and that he will humble himself
under Your mighty hand, that You, God, may
exalt him in due time.

1 PETER 5:5–6

I pray that my son will be like Jesus and humble himself and become obedient.

PHILIPPIANS 2:8

■

I pray that if my son is willing and obedient he shall eat the good of the land.

ISAIAH 1:19

■

I pray that like You, Jesus, my son learns obedience by the things which he suffers.

HEBREWS 5:8

■

I pray that my son does not let sin reign in his mortal body, that he should obey it in its lusts. I also pray that he does not present himself to sin, but that he presents himself to You, God, as being alive from the dead, and his members as instruments of righteousness to God. For sin shall not have dominion over him, for he is not under law but under grace.

ROMANS 6:12–14

I pray that my son knows and understands that no grave trouble will overtake the righteous, but the wicked shall be filled with evil.

PROVERBS 12:21

———— ■ ————

I pray that my son will submit to You, God. That he will resist the devil and he will flee from him.

JAMES 4:7

———— ■ ————

I pray that while my son was once darkness, now he is light in the Lord and that he will walk as a child of the light.

EPHESIANS 5:8

———— ■ ————

I pray that my son will no longer walk in the futility of his mind.

EPHESIANS 4:17

36

SALVATION

Lord, the most important thing in life is salvation. I pray for my son's salvation through the powerful praying of Your Holy Word. Hear these my prayers for my son. Honor them. And bless him with Your salvation. In Jesus' name I pray. Amen.

**God, in accordance
with Your Word . . .**

I pray that my son will discover that Jesus said, "He who believes in Me has everlasting life."

JOHN 6:47

———— ■ ————

I pray that my son remembers that Jesus has come to seek and to save that which was lost.

LUKE 19:10

I pray, Lord Jesus, that my son will come to understand what You meant when You said, "Therefore whoever confesses Me before men, him I will also confess before My Father who is in heaven."

MATTHEW 10:32

---◼---

I pray that if my son will confess with his mouth the Lord Jesus and believe in his heart that God raised Him from the dead, he will be saved. For with his heart he believes to righteousness, and with his mouth confession is made to salvation.

ROMANS 10:9–10

---◼---

I pray that You, God, have saved my son and called him with a holy calling, not according to his works, but according to Your own purpose and grace which was given to him in Christ Jesus before time began.

2 TIMOTHY 1:9

I pray that You, God, so loved my son that
You gave Your only begotten Son, that if my
son believes in Him he should not perish
but have everlasting life.

JOHN 3:16

■

I pray that You did not send Your Son into
the world to condemn my son, but that my
son through Him might be saved.

JOHN 3:17

■

I pray that this will be my son's testimony:
that You, God, have given him eternal life,
and this life is in Your Son.

1 JOHN 5:11

■

I pray that by grace my son has been saved
through faith, and that not of himself; it is
the gift of God, not of works, lest he should
boast.

EPHESIANS 2:8–9

I pray, God, that it is not by works of righteousness which my son has done, but according to Your mercy You saved him, through the washing of regeneration and renewing of the Holy Spirit whom You poured out on him abundantly through Jesus Christ his Savior.

TITUS 3:5–6

I pray, God, that Jesus stands at the door and knocks and if my son hears His voice and opens the door, He will come in to my son and dine with him, and my son with Him.

REVELATION 3:20

I pray, God, that my son has been born again, not of corruptible seed but incorruptible, through Your word which lives and abides forever.

1 PETER 1:23

37

SATAN DEFEATED

Heavenly Father, my son's enemy is Satan. He wants to destroy him. But God, Your word is stronger than even Satan and that is what I pray on my son's behalf. I pray Your word that he will defeat every attack of Satan in his life. God, please honor the praying of Your word to the defeat of Satan in his life. Thank You, God, in the powerful name of Jesus. Amen.

God, in accordance
with Your Word . . .

I pray that my son will be strong in You, Lord, and the power of Your might. I pray that he will put on the whole armor of God, that he may be able to stand against the wiles of the devil. For he does not wrestle against flesh and blood, but against principalities, against powers, against the rulers of the darkness of this age, against spiritual hosts of wickedness in the heavenly places. I pray that he will take up Your whole armor, God, that he may be able to withstand in the evil day, and having done all, to stand. I pray that he has girded his waist with truth, having put on the breastplate of righteousness, and having shod his feet with the preparation of the gospel of peace and above all, taking the shield of faith with which he will be able to quench all the fiery darts of the wicked one. I pray that he also takes the helmet of salvation, and the sword of the Spirit, which is the word of God; praying always with all prayer and supplication in the Spirit, being watchful to this end with all perseverance and supplication for all the saints.

EPHESIANS 6:10–18

■

I pray that You, God, will open my son's eyes, in order to turn him from darkness to light, and from the power of Satan to You, that he may receive forgiveness of sins and an inheritance among those who are sanctified by faith in Jesus.

ACTS 26:18

I pray, God, that You preserve the soul of my son and deliver him out of the hand of the wicked.

PSALM 97:10

I pray, God, for my son that the Son of God was manifested that He might destroy the works of the devil.

1 JOHN 3:8

I pray for my son that he put off, concerning his former conduct, the old man which grows corrupt according to the deceitful lusts, and be renewed in the spirit of his mind and that he put on the new man which was created according to You, God, in true righteousness and holiness.

EPHESIANS 4:22–24

I pray, Jesus, that my son knows that You have disarmed principalities and powers, and

have made a public spectacle of them,
triumphing over them in it.

COLOSSIANS 2:15

■

I pray, God, that my son understands that
even the angels who did not keep their
proper domain, but left their own abode,
You have reserved in everlasting chains
under darkness for the judgment of the great
day.

JUDE 1:6

■

I pray that my son is strong, and that the
word of God abides in him and he has
overcome the wicked one.

1 JOHN 2:14

■

I pray that my son will not give place to the
devil.

EPHESIANS 4:27

I do not pray, God, that You should take my son out of the world, but that You should keep him from the evil one.

JOHN 17:15

———— ■ ————

I pray that my son will submit to You, God, and that he will resist the devil and he will flee from him.

JAMES 4:7

———— ■ ————

I pray that my son will be sober and vigilant, because his adversary the devil walks about like a roaring lion, seeking whom he may devour. I pray that he will resist him, steadfast in the faith, knowing that the same sufferings are experienced by other Christians in the world.

1 PETER 5:8–9

———— ■ ————

I pray that at this time my son will remember that Jesus went about doing good and

healing all who were oppressed by the devil,
for God was with Him.

ACTS 10:38

■

I pray that You, God, have delivered my son
from the power of darkness and conveyed
him into the kingdom of Jesus, in whom he
has redemption through His blood, the
forgiveness of sins.

COLOSSIANS 1:13–14

■

I pray that in all things my son is more than
a conqueror through Him who loved him.

ROMANS 8:37

■

I pray, God, that the accuser of my son, who
accuses him before his God day and night,
has been cast down. I pray that he overcame
him by the blood of the Lamb and by the
word of his testimony.

REVELATION 12:10–11

I pray that while my son is hard pressed on every side, yet not crushed; he is perplexed, but not in despair; persecuted, but not forsaken; struck down, but not destroyed— always carrying about in his body the dying of the Lord Jesus, that the life of Jesus also may be manifested in his body.

2 CORINTHIANS 4:8–10

———— ■ ————

I pray that though my son walks in the flesh, he does not war according to the flesh. For the weapons of his warfare are not carnal but mighty in God for pulling down strongholds, casting down arguments and every high thing that exalts itself against the knowledge of God, bringing every thought into captivity to the obedience of Christ.

2 CORINTHIANS 10:3–5

———— ■ ————

I pray that my son has his senses exercised to discern both good and evil.

HEBREWS 5:14

I pray that neither death nor life, nor angels nor principalities nor powers, nor things present nor things to come, nor height nor depth, nor any other created thing, shall be able to separate my son from the love of God which is in Christ Jesus his Lord.

ROMANS 8:38–39

■

I pray, Lord, that You will guard my son from the evil one.

2 THESSALONIANS 3:3

■

I pray, God, that Your Presence will go with my son forever.

EXODUS 33:14

■

I pray, God, that my son will be strong and of good courage; that he will not be afraid, nor dismayed, for You, the LORD his God, are with him wherever he goes.

JOSHUA 1:9

I pray, God, that You will preserve the soul
of my son and that You will deliver him out
of the hand of the wicked.

PSALM 97:10

———— ■ ————

I pray, God, that You are my son's refuge
and that You will thrust out the enemy from
before him.

DEUTERONOMY 33:27

———— ■ ————

I pray, God, that the angel of the LORD
encamps all around my son who fears You,
and delivers him.

PSALM 34:7

———— ■ ————

I pray that my son will gird up the loins of
his mind and be sober, and rest his hope
fully upon the grace that is to be brought
to him at the revelation of Jesus Christ, as

an obedient child, not conforming himself
to the former lusts, as in his ignorance; but
as You, God, who called him are holy, may
he also be holy in all his conduct.

1 PETER 1:13–15

———— ■ ————

I pray that my son will have the mind of
Christ.

1 CORINTHIANS 2:16

———— ■ ————

I pray that Satan will not take advantage of
my son for he is not ignorant of his devices.

2 CORINTHIANS 2:11

———— ■ ————

I pray that my son knows that he does not
live by bread alone but by every word that
proceeds from the mouth of God.

MATTHEW 4:4

I pray, Lord, that my son will drive Satan
away by worshiping the Lord his God, and
Him only he shall serve.

MATTHEW 4:10

38

SECURITY

Lord, real and true security comes only from You. I pray Your words concerning security for my son. Help him to sense the security that only You can give. Lord, I thank You and I pray in Your name. Amen.

God, in accordance
with Your Word . . .

I pray that my son is persuaded that neither death nor life, nor angels nor principalities nor powers, nor things present nor things to come, nor height nor depth, nor any other created thing, shall be able to separate him from the love of God which is in Christ Jesus his Lord.

ROMANS 8:38–39

■

I pray that in Jesus my son also trusted, after he heard the word of truth, the gospel of

his salvation, in whom also, having believed,
he was sealed with the Holy Spirit of
promise.

EPHESIANS 1:13

■

I pray that surely goodness and mercy shall
follow my son all the days of his life and
that he will dwell in the house of the LORD
forever.

PSALM 23:6

■

I pray that my son is one of those who has
come to You, Jesus, and who You will by
no means cast out.

JOHN 6:37

■

I pray, Jesus, that my son has heard Your
voice and that You know him, and that he
follows You and that You will give him
eternal life, and he shall never perish.

JOHN 10:27–28

I pray that my son does not grieve the Holy
Spirit of God, by whom he was sealed for
the day of redemption.

EPHESIANS 4:30

———— ■ ————

I pray that You, God, who have begun a
good work in my son will complete it until
the day of Jesus Christ.

PHILIPPIANS 1:6

———— ■ ————

I pray, Lord, that Your faithfulness will
establish my son and guard him from the
evil one.

2 THESSALONIANS 3:3

———— ■ ————

I pray that You, God, are able to keep my
son from stumbling and to present him
faultless before the presence of Your glory
with exceeding joy.

JUDE 1:24

39

SERVING GOD

Lord God, in accordance with Your perfect word I pray that my son will walk after You and that he will serve You. Your word is clear that he cannot serve two masters. I ask You to use Your Holy Spirit to guide him and direct him in this area of his life in accordance with Your word. Thank You in Jesus' name. Amen.

God, in accordance with Your Word . . .

I pray that my son will walk after You, the LORD his God, and fear You, and keep Your commandments and obey Your voice, and that he shall serve You and hold fast to You.

DEUTERONOMY 13:4

———— ■ ————

I pray, God, that my son knows that he cannot serve two masters; for either he will hate the one and love the other, or else he will be loyal to the one and despise the other. He cannot serve You and mammon.

MATTHEW 6:24

———— ■ ————

I pray that my son will worship You, the Lord his God, and You only he shall serve.

MATTHEW 4:10

———— ■ ————

I pray that my son will love You, the LORD his God, and walk in all Your ways, keeping Your commandments, and holding fast to You, and serving You with all his heart and with all his soul.

JOSHUA 22:5

———— ■ ————

I pray to You, God, that my son will present his body a living sacrifice, holy, acceptable to You, which is his reasonable service. I pray also that he will not be conformed to this world, but be transformed by the renewing of his mind, that he may prove what is that good and acceptable and perfect will of Yours.

ROMANS 12:1–2

———— ■ ————

I pray that my son will be kindly affectionate to others with brotherly love, in honor giving preference to others; not lagging in diligence, fervent in spirit, serving You, Lord; rejoicing in hope, patient in tribulation, continuing steadfastly in prayer; distributing to the needs of the saints, given to hospitality.

ROMANS 12:10–13

———— ■ ————

I pray, O God, that my son shall serve You, the LORD his God.

EXODUS 23:25

———— ■ ————

I pray that my son will fear You, the LORD his God, and walk in all Your ways and love You, and serve You, the LORD his God, with

all his heart and with all his soul and that
he will keep Your commandments and Your
statutes which You command him today for
his good.

DEUTERONOMY 10:12–13

■

I pray that my son does not turn aside from
following You, LORD, but serves You with all
his heart. I pray that he does not turn aside,
for then he would go after empty things
which cannot profit or deliver, for they are
nothing. For You will not forsake him, for
Your great name's sake, because it has
pleased You to make him Yours.

1 SAMUEL 12:20–22

■

I pray that my son will know You, God, and
serve You with a loyal heart and with a
willing mind; for You search all hearts and
understand all the intent of the thoughts. If
he seeks You, You will be found by him; but

if he forsakes You, You will cast him off forever.

1 CHRONICLES 28:9

———— ■ ————

I pray that my son has been delivered from the law, having died to what he was held by, so that he should serve in the newness of the Spirit and not in the oldness of the letter.

ROMANS 7:6

———— ■ ————

I pray that my son will serve You, LORD, with gladness and that he will come before Your presence with singing. I pray that he will know that You, LORD, are God and that it is You who has made him, and not he himself.

PSALM 100:2–3

40

SICKNESS

Heavenly Father, in accordance with the perfection of Your word I pray that You will heal my son of his affliction and restore his health. We need Your help and pray Your word for that important need to be met. It is in the powerful name of Jesus that I pray these prayers to You. Amen.

God, in accordance with Your Word . . .

I pray that You will heal my son, O LORD, and he shall be healed. Save him and he shall be saved.

JEREMIAH 17:14

———— ■ ————

I pray, God, that You will restore health to my son and heal his wounds.

JEREMIAH 30:17

I pray that my son will diligently heed Your voice, LORD God, and do what is right in Your sight and give ear to Your commandments and keep all Your statutes, and that You will put no diseases on him.

EXODUS 15:26

———— ■ ————

I pray, O God, that because Jesus was wounded for my son's transgressions and He was bruised for his iniquities, that by His stripes he is healed.

ISAIAH 53:5

———— ■ ————

I pray, God, that You heal all my son's diseases and redeem his life from destruction.

PSALM 103:3–4

———— ■ ————

I pray that my son may prosper in all things and be in health, just as his soul prospers.

3 JOHN 1:2

I pray that Jesus Himself bore my son's sins in His own body on the tree, and that he, having died to sin, might live for righteousness—by whose stripes he was healed.

1 PETER 2:24

■

I pray, O God, that my son remembers that Jesus healed every sickness and every disease among the people.

MATTHEW 9:35

■

I pray, Jesus, that power goes out from You and heals my son.

LUKE 6:19

■

I pray, God, that You have sent Your word and healed my son and delivered him from destruction.

PSALM 107:20

I pray, God, that I am not worthy that You
should come under my roof. But only speak
a word, and my son will be healed.

MATTHEW 8:8

———— ■ ————

I pray that the prayer of faith will save my
son from his sickness and that You, Lord,
will raise him up. And if he has committed
sins, he will be forgiven.

JAMES 5:15

41

SPIRITUAL GROWTH

Lord Jesus, there is no more powerful prayer that I can pray than to pray the word of God directly from the pages of the Bible. That is what I now do as I pray for my son's spiritual growth. I pray that my son will take heed to himself and keep himself in accordance with Your word. Thank You for honoring Your words that I pray to You now. Amen.

**God, in accordance
with Your Word . . .**

I pray that my son will beware, lest there
be in him an evil heart of unbelief in
departing from the living God. I pray that I
will exhort him daily, while it is called
"Today," lest he be hardened through the
deceitfulness of sin.

HEBREWS 3:12–13

I pray that my son does not forget You, the LORD his God, by not keeping Your commandments, Your judgments, and Your statutes which You command him today. I pray that he shall remember the LORD his God, for it is You who give him the power to get wealth.

DEUTERONOMY 8:11, 18

■

I pray that my son has not forgotten the name of his God, or stretched out his hands to a foreign god. Would You, God, not search this out? For You know the secrets of the heart.

PSALM 44:20–21

■

I pray that after my son has escaped the pollutions of the world through the knowledge of his Lord and Savior Jesus Christ, that he not become entangled in them and overcome.

2 PETER 2:20

I pray that my son will take heed to himself,
and diligently keep himself, lest he forget
the things his eyes have seen, and lest they
depart from his heart all the days of his life.

DEUTERONOMY 4:9

— ■ —

I pray, God, that my son returns to You, and
You will return to him.

MALACHI 3:7

— ■ —

I pray that my son will look diligently lest
he fall short of Your grace, God, and lest any
root of bitterness spring up causing trouble,
and by this he become defiled.

HEBREWS 12:15

— ■ —

I pray, God, that my son will be watchful,
and strengthen the things which remain, that
are ready to die, for he has not found his
works perfect before You.

REVELATION 3:2

42

STRENGTH

God, I call upon You now to give my son more strength than ever before. I pray that You will increase his strength according to Your word. In Jesus' precious name I pray. Amen.

God, in accordance with Your Word . . .

I pray, God, that You give power to my son, who is weak, and that You increase his strength.

ISAIAH 40:29

———————— ■ ————————

I pray that my son shall wait on You, LORD, and that he shall renew his strength. I pray that he shall mount up with wings like eagles, that he shall run and not be weary and that he shall walk and not faint.

ISAIAH 40:31

I pray that my son will fear not, for You are with him. I pray that he will be not dismayed, for You are his God. You will strengthen him and help him and You will uphold him with Your righteous right hand.

ISAIAH 41:10

———— ■ ————

I pray that You, LORD, are my son's rock and his fortress and his deliverer; his God, his strength, in whom he will trust; his shield and the horn of his salvation, his stronghold. I pray that he will call upon You, LORD, who are worthy to be praised; so shall he be saved from his enemies.

PSALM 18:2–3

———— ■ ————

I pray that my son will be strong in You, Lord, and in the power of Your might. I pray that he will put on the whole armor of God, that he may be able to stand against the wiles of the devil. For he does not wrestle against flesh and blood, but against principalities, against powers, against the

rulers of the darkness of this age, against
spiritual hosts of wickedness in the heavenly
places.

EPHESIANS 6:10–12

———— ■ ————

I pray that You, LORD, are my son's light and
his salvation. Whom shall he fear?

PSALM 27:1

———— ■ ————

I pray, God, that You will strengthen my son
according to Your word.

PSALM 119:28

———— ■ ————

I pray that my son will take up Your whole
armor, God, that he may be able to
withstand in the evil day, and having done
all, to stand. I pray that he will stand
therefore, having girded his waist with truth,
having put on the breastplate of
righteousness, and having shod his feet with
the preparation of the gospel of peace; above

all, taking the shield of faith with which he will be able to quench all the fiery darts of the wicked one. I pray also that he will take the helmet of salvation, and the sword of the Spirit, which is the word of God, praying always with all prayer and supplication in the Spirit.

EPHESIANS 6:13–18

———— ■ ————

I pray that my son will be strengthened with all might, according to Your glorious power, God.

COLOSSIANS 1:11

———— ■ ————

I pray that my son can do all things through Christ who strengthens him.

PHILIPPIANS 4:13

———— ■ ————

I pray that You, God, will grant my son, according to the riches of Your glory, to be strengthened with might through Your Spirit.

EPHESIANS 3:16

43

TEMPTED

Jesus, Your word says that You know how to deliver my son out of temptations. I pray right now that You will now and forevermore deliver the son that I love so much from any temptation that he may encounter. I pray Your word for him in this area, and I trust You to do as Your word promises. In Your name I pray. Amen.

God, in accordance with Your Word . . .

I pray that You, Lord, know how to deliver my son out of temptations.

2 PETER 2:9

—————— ■ ——————

I pray that sin shall not have dominion over my son, for he is not under law but under grace.

ROMANS 6:14

I pray, Lord, that Your word my son has hidden in his heart, that he might not sin against You.

PSALM 119:11

———— ■ ————

I pray that if my son confesses and forsakes his sins he will have mercy.

PROVERBS 28:13

———— ■ ————

I pray that if my son confesses his sins, You are faithful and just to forgive his sins and to cleanse him from all unrighteousness.

1 JOHN 1:9

———— ■ ————

I pray, Lord, that my son will not say when he is tempted, "I am tempted by God"; for You cannot be tempted by evil, nor do You Yourself tempt anyone. For he is tempted when he is drawn away by his own desires and enticed. Then, when desire has conceived, it gives birth to sin; and sin, when

it is full-grown, brings forth death. I pray
that my son will not be deceived.

JAMES 1:13–16

———— ■ ————

I pray that no temptation has overtaken my
son except such as is common to man; but
You, God, are faithful and will not allow him
to be tempted beyond what he is able, but
with the temptation You will also make the
way of escape, that he may be able to bear
it.

1 CORINTHIANS 10:13

———— ■ ————

I pray that my son does not have a High
Priest who cannot sympathize with his
weaknesses, but was in all points tempted
as he is, yet without sin. Let him therefore
come boldly to the throne of grace, that he
may obtain mercy and find grace to help
in time of need.

HEBREWS 4:15–16

I pray, Jesus, that You are able to aid my
son who is tempted.

HEBREWS 2:18

———— ■ ————

I pray that my son will be sober and vigilant;
because his adversary the devil walks about
like a roaring lion, seeking whom he may
devour. I pray that he will resist him,
steadfast in the faith, knowing that the same
sufferings are experienced by his Christian
brothers in the world.

1 PETER 5:8–9

———— ■ ————

I pray that my son will be strong in You,
Lord, and in Your might. I pray that he will
put on Your whole armor, that he may be
able to stand against the wiles of the devil
and that above all, he takes the shield of
faith with which he will be able to quench
all the fiery darts of the wicked one.

EPHESIANS 6:10–11, 16

I pray, God, that my son will resist the devil
and the devil will flee from him.

JAMES 4:7

———— ■ ————

I pray, Lord, that my son will count it all
joy when he falls into various trials, knowing
that the testing of his faith produces patience.
I pray that blessed is my son who endures
temptation; for when he has been approved,
he will receive the crown of life which You
have promised to those who love You.

JAMES 1:2–3, 12

———— ■ ————

I pray that You, God, are able to keep my
son from stumbling, and to present him
faultless before the presence of Your glory
with exceeding joy.

JUDE 1:24

———— ■ ————

I pray that in this my son will greatly rejoice,
though now for a little while, if need be, he

has been grieved by various trials, that the genuineness of his faith, being much more precious than gold that perishes, though it is tested by fire, may be found to praise, honor, and glory at the revelation of Jesus Christ.

1 PETER 1:6–7

———— ◾ ————

I pray, God, that He who is in my son is greater than he who is in the world.

1 JOHN 4:4

44

TROUBLES

Lord, Your word says that You will allow no more troubles than my son can bear. Today, even now, I pray Your word to overcome any troubles my son may have. Please honor Your words as my prayers and take care of and strengthen him. It is in the authority of the name of Jesus that I pray. Amen.

God, in accordance with Your Word . . .

I pray that my son shall obtain joy and gladness and that sorrow and sighing shall flee away.

ISAIAH 51:11

———— ■ ————

I pray that my son will be anxious for nothing, but in everything by prayer and supplication, with thanksgiving, will let his requests be made known to You, God, and

that Your peace, which surpasses all
understanding, will guard his heart and mind
through Christ Jesus.

PHILIPPIANS 4:6–7

■

I pray, God, that You will comfort my son
in all his tribulation, that he may be able
to comfort those who are in any trouble,
with the comfort with which he himself is
comforted by You.

2 CORINTHIANS 1:4

■

I pray, God, that my son does not worry
about tomorrow, for tomorrow will worry
about its own things.

MATTHEW 6:34

■

I pray that all things work together for good
to my son who loves You, God, to him who
is called according to Your purpose.

ROMANS 8:28

I pray that my son will be glad and rejoice in Your mercy, for You have considered his trouble. You have known his soul in adversities, and have not shut him up into the hand of the enemy; You have set his feet in a wide place.

PSALM 31:7–8

———— ■ ————

I pray that my son's help comes from You, LORD, who made heaven and earth.

PSALM 121:2

———— ■ ————

I pray that my son will come boldly to the throne of grace, that he may obtain mercy and find grace to help in time of need.

HEBREWS 4:16

———— ■ ————

I pray, God, that my son will cast all his cares upon You, for You care for him.

1 PETER 5:7

I pray, O God, that my son always
remembers that You are good, a stronghold
in his day of trouble; and that You know that
he trusts in You.

NAHUM 1:7

■

I pray that though my son is hard pressed
on every side, he is not crushed; he is
perplexed, but not in despair; persecuted,
but not forsaken; struck down, but not
destroyed.

2 CORINTHIANS 4:8–9

■

I pray that my son will not let his heart be
troubled. I pray that he believes in You, God,
and also in Jesus.

JOHN 14:1

■

I pray, God, that when my son passes
through the waters, You will be with him.
And through the rivers, they shall not

overflow him. When he walks through the fire, he shall not be burned, nor shall the flame scorch him.

ISAIAH 43:2

———— ■ ————

I pray that though my son walks in the midst of trouble, You, God, will revive him. You will stretch out Your hand against the wrath of his enemies, and Your right hand will save him.

PSALM 138:7

45

WAITING ON GOD

Heavenly Father, I really do believe that the most important thing that I can do is to pray Your very words and thoughts over my son. My prayers today will be Your words from Your word. Hear my prayers and help my son to wait on You. I pray everything in Jesus' wonderful name. Amen.

God, in accordance
with Your Word . . .

I pray, God, that my son will say in that day: "Behold, this is my God; I have waited for Him, and He will save me. This is the LORD; I have waited for Him. I will be glad and rejoice in His salvation."

ISAIAH 25:9

———— ■ ————

I pray that my son's soul waits for You, LORD, that You are his help and his shield.

PSALM 33:20

I pray that my son has become a partaker
of Christ if he holds the beginning of his
confidence steadfast to the end.

HEBREWS 3:14

I pray that my son waits for You, LORD, that
his soul waits, and in Your word he does
hope.

PSALM 130:5

I pray that my son will wait on You, LORD,
and that he will be of good courage. I pray
also that You will strengthen his heart.

PSALM 27:14

I pray, God, that my son's soul waits silently
for You alone and that his expectation is
from You.

PSALM 62:5

I pray, O God, that my son will hold fast to
the confession of his hope without wavering,
for You who promised are faithful.

HEBREWS 10:23

---■---

I pray that my son shall wait on You, LORD,
and that he shall renew his strength. I pray
also that he shall mount up with wings like
eagles and that he shall run and not be
weary, and walk and not faint.

ISAIAH 40:31

46

WORRIED

Most Precious God, You have promised to not let my son's heart be troubled if he will cast his cares on You. Based on Your words I pray that all worry will flee from him and that his joy will return to him. All of my prayers I pray in Jesus' name. Amen.

God, in accordance
with Your Word . . .

I pray, God, that my son will not let his heart be troubled.

JOHN 14:1

———— ■ ————

I pray that my son will lie down in peace, and sleep; for You alone, O LORD, make him dwell in safety.

PSALM 4:8

I pray that my son will cast all his cares upon You, God, for You care for him.

1 PETER 5:7

———— ■ ————

I pray that You, God, will keep my son in perfect peace, he whose mind is stayed on You, because he trusts in You.

ISAIAH 26:3

———— ■ ————

I pray, God, that my son will let Your peace rule in his heart.

COLOSSIANS 3:15

———— ■ ————

I pray that my son will be anxious for nothing, but in everything by prayer and supplication, with thanksgiving, let his requests be made known to You, God, and that Your peace, which surpasses all understanding, will guard his heart and mind in Christ Jesus.

PHILIPPIANS 4:6–7

I pray, God, that You shall supply all my son's needs according to Your riches in glory by Christ Jesus.

PHILIPPIANS 4:19

I pray that my son will not worry about his life, what he will eat or what he will drink; nor about his body, what he will put on. I pray that he will seek first Your kingdom, God, and Your righteousness, and all these things shall be added to him.

MATTHEW 6:25, 33

I pray, Lord, that when my son lies down, he will not be afraid. I pray that he will lie down and his sleep will be sweet.

PROVERBS 3:24

I pray that my son will say of You, LORD, "He is my refuge and my fortress; my God, in Him I will trust."

PSALM 91:2

I pray, O God, that great peace has my son
who loves Your law, and nothing can cause
him to stumble.

PSALM 119:165

■

I pray, Jesus, that Your peace You leave with
my son and that Your peace You give to him;
not as the world gives do You give to him.
Let not his heart be troubled, neither let it
be afraid.

JOHN 14:27

———————— ~❦~ ————————

Seminars conducted by Lee Roberts include *Praying God's Will, Avoiding Failure in Your Christian Walk,* and *The Businessman, the Salesman, and God!*

More information on these seminars can be obtained by writing Lee Roberts, P.O. Box 671465, Marietta, GA 30067-0025, or by calling 404-956-8550.